GUITAR *signature licks*

BEST OF SURF GUITAR

By Dave Rubin

ISBN 0-634-07364-8

HAL•LEONARD® CORPORATION

7777 W. BLUEMOUND RD. P.O. BOX 13819 MILWAUKEE, WI 53213

Copyright © 2004 by HAL LEONARD CORPORATION
International Copyright Secured   All Rights Reserved

For all works contained herein:
Unauthorized copying, arranging, adapting, recording or
public performance is an infringement of copyright.
Infringers are liable under the law.

Visit Hal Leonard Online at
www.halleonard.com

CONTENTS

Page	Title	CD Track
4	Dedication	
4	Introduction	
	Tuning	1
7	**Let's Go Trippin'**	2–6
10	**Mr. Moto**	7–10
13	**Out of Limits**	11–13
16	**Penetration**	14–16
20	**Pipeline**	17–19
26	**Shake 'n' Stomp**	20–25
30	**Surf City**	26–28
33	**Surfin' Safari**	29–32
36	**Surfin' U.S.A.**	33–38
39	**The Wedge**	39–42
44	Guitar Notation Legend	

DEDICATION

I would like to dedicate this book to my daughter Michelle and my wife Cheryl. While they are not huge surf music fans like me, they do love the beach, which I can take or leave. I would also like to thank Ira Bolterman, Darrell Bridges, and Marta Bulaich (a real "California Girl") for their help and support.

INTRODUCTION

Surf Guitar: Cowabunga, Gnarly Hodads!

One of the many late and lamented subgenres of rock 'n' roll to come out of the 1950s was instrumental music. Postwar R&B had produced instrumental hits like "Night Train" (1951) by tenor saxophonist Jimmy Forrest, and swing jazz before that was based upon nonvocal dance numbers such as Benny Goodman's "Don't Be That Way" (#1 in 1938) and Glenn Miller's "In the Mood" (#1 in 1940). Then in 1956 Hammond B-3 organist Bill Doggett scored a #2 hit (just behind Elvis's #1 "Heartbreak Hotel") with "Honky Tonk," featuring the sublimely jazzy bluesman Billy Butler on guitar, and the potential of instrumentals was glimpsed at the dawn of the rock era. Beginning with Duane Eddy in 1957 and for the next half dozen years or so, the Top 40 airwaves would jangle with the joyous sounds of (mostly blues-based) guitar melodies and hooks. Duane Eddy, the Ventures, Johnny and the Hurricanes, Link Wray, and the Champs, among countless others, kept the exuberant, even rowdy nature of rock 'n' roll alive against all odds during the drab period of sappy pop music as typified by Frankie Avalon and Fabian, and lame folk music disguised as hootenanny. Starting in the early 1960s, surf music would give instrumental rock a new, if short-lived, lease on life. Eddy's influence, in particular, cannot be overestimated, as his reverbed bass string melodies laid the groundwork for an oceanful of hits.

Though surfing had been a Southern California tradition since being introduced by the Hawaiian-Irishman George Freeth in 1907, two separate but related occurrences would be necessary to bring the sport and the formation of its signature music together. In 1959 a silly beach movie called *Gidget* showed an appealing, hedonistic lifestyle featuring surfing (and the attendant babes that it attracted) that intrigued the emerging youth culture throughout the country. Concurrently, Dick Dale had been performing for a couple of years in local ballrooms around Newport Beach while also becoming an avid surfer— a factor of major importance to the development of his music as he would try to actually recreate the sound of waves crashing around him that he heard while out on his board. Initially Dale played country and western and big band music with his Rhythm Wranglers, but as his audience evolved to include surfers and other beach kids, he began to rock it 'n' roll it. Like Duane Eddy, he "loved Louis Armstrong" and had started on the trumpet before switching to guitar, but from 1957–59 he was relegated to playing trumpet in a country and western band. From 1958–60 he recorded a handful of vocal/guitar singles on Del-Tone Records, the company formed by his father, that show a surprisingly hefty R&B influence (a crucial component of much surf music) rather than country and western. Most significantly, however, Dale started playing with his proto-surf band, the Del-Tones, at the Rinky Dink Ice Cream Parlor in Newport Beach in 1959. When they quickly outgrew the ice cream parlor and took up residence at the cavernous Rendezvous Ballroom not far away, the birth of an era was at hand.

Technically, Dale's signature sound was largely the result of a swing era drummer and cutting edge tube amp technology. He says, "I listened to Gene Krupa on my father's 78 RPM records. I loved his drumming because it was like sex, and I got my approach to rhythm from him. In the late fifties you were limited by the size of your amp. I worked with Leo Fender, blowing up over sixty amps, until we came up with the Dual Showman that would stand up to my heavy picking."

An extremely enterprising individual regarding self-promotion and the pioneering of an electric guitar revolution, Dale always had a keen interest in improving his sound. The marriage between the Fender Dual Showman amplifier and Dale's Fender Stratocaster in 1961 would prove to be a good and lasting one. The final and perhaps critical element in the development of the "Dick Dale sound" and the instrumental surf sound in general, however, was the outboard reverb tank. Originally Dale felt he needed something to enhance his singing voice when it was the featured component of his music at the time, and Fender gave him a prototype licensed from the Hammond Organ Company to try out. When he happened to plug his Strat in as an experiment he quickly realized that this was the proper application for the device. Before long the teenagers—not Dale or even the other surf musicians—would christen his music the "Dick Dale surfin' sound." Apparently it was surfers themselves who started making the connection between the watery sound of trebly Fender guitars awash in reverb and the sound of "hanging ten" while waves crashed around them. It should be noted that none other than Jimi Hendrix was influenced and inspired by Dick Dale. The future Voodoo Child was on tour with Little Richard in 1965 when he met Dale and allegedly questioned the surf guitar guru extensively. When Dale was hospitalized with cancer in 1966 Hendrix was in the process of recording *Are You Experienced?* and dedicated the instrumental "Third Stone from the Sun" to him by injecting "You'll never hear surf music again" into the recording, thinking the Strat-mauler was dying. Fortunately for all, Dale recovered and is still torturing his strings to the day of this writing.

A harmonic convergence would occur in 1961, a good year for cool custom color electric Fender guitars and hot Chevy Impalas, as a technicolor shade was drawn on the gray, conservative 1950s, and popular culture looked West. In 1959 Southern California schoolmates Paul Johnson and Eddie Bertrand, like Bob Bogle and Don Wilson of the Ventures up North, had discovered a common interest in the guitar and began playing Duane Eddy and Johnny & the Hurricanes instrumentals. A year later they formed the Belairs and recorded "Mr. Moto," arguably the first surf instrumental, in April of 1961 (though Johnson is quick to point out that "Underwater" by the Frogmen—produced by the ubiquitous Joe Saraceno—preceded "Mr. Moto" by a month). That summer Johnson made a pilgrimage to the Rendezvous Ballroom on Balboa Island to catch Dick Dale and the Del-Tones. Dale's overwhelming staccato technique and thunderous volume combined with the hordes of surfers stomping on the ballroom floor made quite an impression on Johnson and all the other local musicians who stopped by to gawk. His shows became legendary events called "stomps" and spawned the group dance known as the "surfer's stomp." "Let's Go Trippin'" (a reference to surfing, not the taking of psychedelic drugs) was Dale's first single in September 1961. It only reached #60, and a year later the monumental "Miserlou," an instrumental version of the 1930 Nikos Roubanis composition (spelled "Misirlou") with its brawny, pick-melting (literally!), double-picked Arabic Hijaz Kar melody and springy reverb did not even chart, but stands as a virtuosic performance in a field often dominated by merely competent guitarists. Its threatening mood was employed to great effect in *Pulp Fiction* in 1994 and revived Dale's ongoing career. "Shake 'n' Stomp" (1962) and "The Wedge" (1963) were two of his last singles before his commercial "wipe-out" in the mid-1960s.

"Pipeline," released by the Chantays in December of 1962 (#4), is for many the embodiment of sun, surf, and sand. With Brian Carman's Bo Diddley-esque gliss and rubbery, muted bass strings, its somber ambience provided by Bob Spickard's minor key melody, and overall reverbed density give the aural equivalent of shooting the curl inside a tube of cascading ocean. It opened a floodgate of surf bands like the Pyramids ("Penetration"), who were directly inspired by it, and studio groups like the Marketts ("Out of Limits"), helping to prolong the "endless summer" up to the British Invasion in 1964. Coincidentally, the English troops also included instrumental groups like the Shadows and the Tornados, who likewise succumbed to the pop onslaught.

Less heralded by guitarists, but a crucial part of the surf saga, is the story of the vocal bands that coexisted in Southern California with the instrumental groups. Dick Dale and his peers referred to their music as "surfing songs" to distinguish it from surf music. Spearheaded by the eponymously named Beach Boys, they of course enjoyed far more commercial success than their fellow Fender-twanging peers. The Beach Boys were led by the brilliant but troubled Brian Wilson, along with his brothers Carl and Dennis, and rounded out by their cousin Mike Love and high school friend Al Jardine. Brian's love for the lush, silky-smooth vocal harmony of the Four Freshmen combined with Carl's admiration for Chuck Berry produced a winning sound first heard nationally on "Surfin' Safari" in the summer of 1962. They followed it with the similar "Surfin' U.S.A" in early 1963 and their first #1 hit, "I Get Around," in 1964. Brian would eventually retire from performing to concentrate on producing the ambitious music for the Beach Boys that he heard in his head, culminating with his artistic masterpiece, *Pet Sounds*, in 1966. Though critically and commercially hailed around the world (particularly in England), it remained stuck in a calm in the U.S. When the Beatles, who Brian felt to be his competition, released *Sgt. Pepper's Lonely Hearts Club Band* the following year to unanimous acclaim, it combined with his drug-addled psyche to push him towards a period of isolation from the band and music that lasted for years.

Jan (Berry) & Dean (Torrance) followed in the wake (pun intended!) of the Beach Boys after playing some shows with them in 1963. Though the duo had been performing with limited success since 1958 (their doo-wop classic "Baby Talk" hit #10 in 1959), when Brian gave them the unfinished "Surf City" and then sang harmony on the single, it made a big splash at #1 in the spring of 1963. In 1964 Jan and Dean also released "Dead Man's Curve" which, like their previous "Drag City," was meant to capitalize on the car song subgenre epitomized by Beach Boys favorites like "409," "Little Deuce Coupe," and "Shut Down" that appeared as the B sides of their early singles. For Jan & Dean, however, the song's grim subject matter would prove tragically prophetic as Jan Berry was nearly killed by a crash in his Corvette Stingray on L.A.'s Mulholland Drive in 1966. Years of rehab were necessary to allow him to even walk and talk again. Over time he and Dean Torrance were able to sing and tour again, but their moment in the sun and considerable contribution (twenty-eight charting singles) was past.

A brief "surf revival" occurred between 1979 and 1982 in Southern California with the Surf Raiders, the Malibooz, Jon & the Nightriders, and the Surf Punks. Along with the Raybeats and the current instrumental champs Los Straitjackets, they showed not only the continuing vitality of the music but the loyal fanbase it still commands. Dick Dale still tours and occasionally records with the same locomotive energy he always possessed. It may be the era of the pop singer, rap, and "emo rock," but for gnarly dudes the sun never sets on a catchy minor key melody and a sproingy eighth-note rhythm awash in deep reverb.

LET'S GO TRIPPIN'
By Dick Dale
Recorded by Dick Dale in 1961

The issue of whether he was the inventor of surf music or the first to record it is pretty much an academic exercise at this point. What is certain, however, is that Dick Dale is and has been the premier surf guitarist for forty-five years and is still capable of melting his picks and burning the strings off his Strat with undiminished aggression. All hail the once and future "King of Surf Guitar!"

Dick Dale was born Richard Mansour on May 4, 1937 in Boston, Massachusetts to a Lebanese father and a Polish mother, but grew up in Southern California. He would incorporate aspects of both ethnicities in his music along with other Mediterranean and Middle Eastern cultures as heard most noticeably in "Miserlou." Through 1966, when he had a life-threatening medical condition interrupt his career, Dale was truly *King of the Surf Guitar* as his 1963 album was aptly titled. His first new album in years, *Tribal Thunder*, came out in 1993, and when "Miserlou" was prominently featured on the soundtrack of *Pulp Fiction* in 1994 he was once again recognized as a hip musical guru.

Figure 1 – Rehearsal Letter A

The intro to "Let's Go Trippin'" betrays vestiges of Dale's country and western past in the 1950s before he became a surfer and had his life changed. After a steady ascending glissando to the root (E) on string 4 at fret 14, he plays a jaunty broken E major barre chord pattern in measures 1–3 that feels like a country two-beat rhythm. In measure 4 he abruptly arpeggiates the E chord combined with the 2nd (F♯) and 6th (C♯) notes from the E major scale, setting the tone for the rest of the instrumental.

Fig. 1

Copyright © 1961 Surf Beat Music (ASCAP)
Copyright Renewed
All Rights Reserved   Used by Permission

Figure 2 – Rehearsal Letter B

Following Letter A, "Let's Go Trippin'" is a series of 12-bar blues choruses (Letters B–F) with the "slow change" (four measures of the I before the change to the IV chord). In measures 1–4 and 7–8 (I chord, E) Dale alternates measures with a broken E major barre chord (similar to measure 3 of Letter A) followed by an arpeggio (similar to measure 4 of Letter A) for a two-measure phrase. In measures 5–6 over the IV chord (A) he relocates to fret 5 and executes similar patterns relative to the key of A. For the V chord (B) in measure 9 and the IV chord in measure 10 Dale combines elements from both measures of the phrase to create two new patterns relative to each chord change and their position on the fingerboard. In measure 11 (I) he breaks up the E major barre chord similarly to measure 7. Interestingly, in measure 12 (V) he appears to breeze right past the harmony (though the bass hits the root of the B chord) and plays the root (E) of the I chord instead, followed by the 3rd/root (G#/E) dyad leading into Rehearsal Letter C (not shown). A happy accident? Perhaps!

Performance Tip: The dynamics between the ringing broken chords and the raked arpeggios is central to the musicality of the tune. Dale would go on to be lauded for his amazing right-hand technique that pummeled his strings like a tsunami, but that was not yet the case. Instead, be aware that you must whip your left hand pinky finger onto the 2nd and 6th notes with all haste in order to stay in time. As in Rehearsal Letter A, form a full barre chord in measures 1, 3, 5, 7, 9, 10, 11, and 12. In measures 2, 4, 6, and 8 shift to the partial barre starting with your ring finger on string 4.

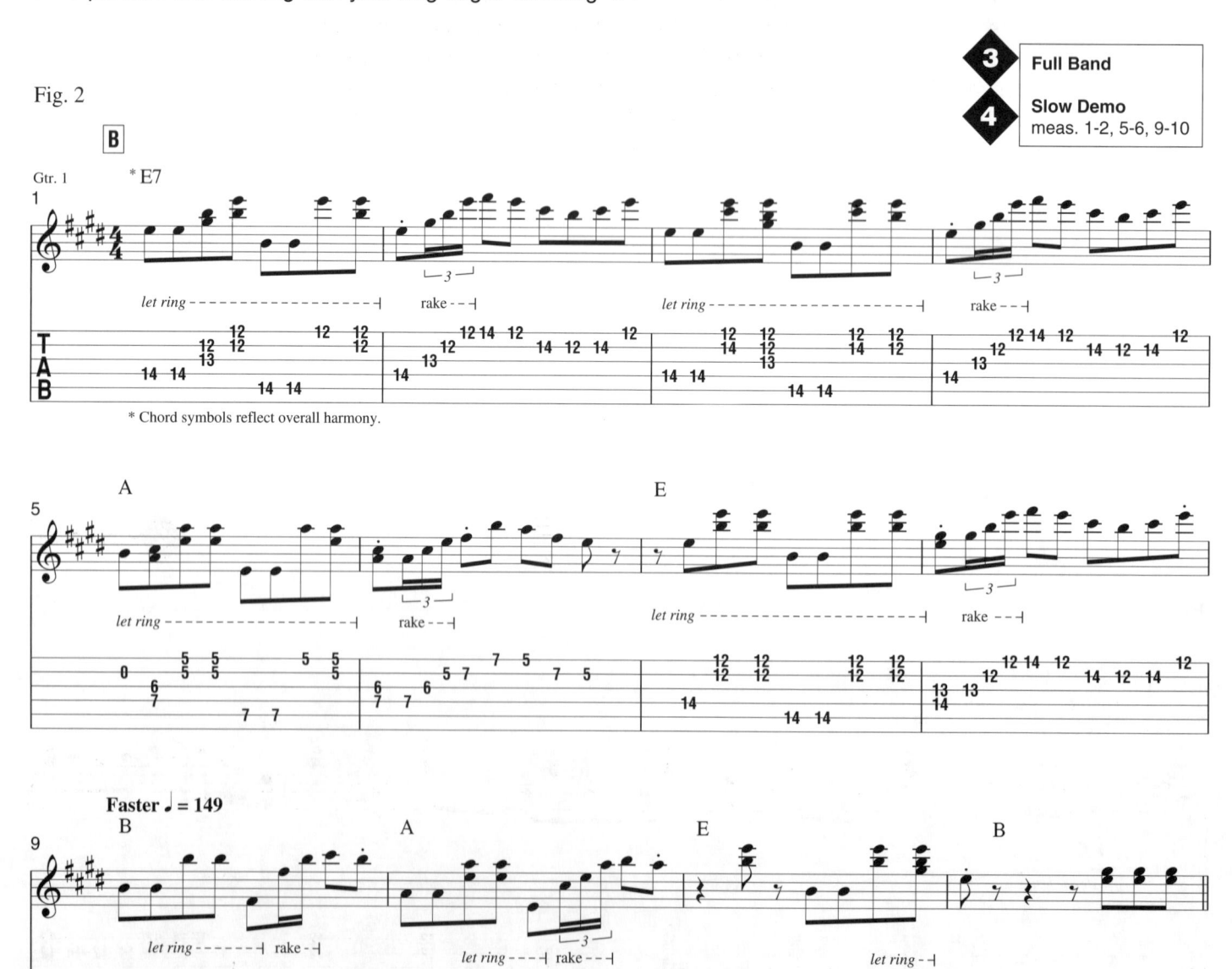

Figure 3 – Rehearsal Letter D

By the time Dale got to Letter D he had moved on to another set of chord forms to follow each change. Though not a "blues guy" by any stretch of the imagination, he was aware of R&B and had played it in his earlier days along with country and western. This is evident here not only in the dominant seventh chord choices, but in the syncopation that tends to accent the double stops on the backbeats of "2" and "4." For the I chord (E7) in measures 1–4, 7–8, and 11–12 Dale plays an E7/B voicing at fret 7 (with the root on string 5) and picks it in a broken chord fashion. In measures 5–6 (IV) he grabs a barre chord at fret 5 and likewise skips over the strings. As in Letter B, Dale invents a different pattern for the V (B) and IV (A) chord changes in measures 9 and 10, respectively. Both contain raked arpeggios with the addition of the 2nd and 6th notes relative to each change, but in a more rolling ascending and descending pattern than the ones in Letter B. Observe that the guitar in measure 12 remains on the I chord (along with the bass) rather than moving to the V.

Performance Tip: In order to efficiently play the E7 voicings, it is recommended that you form the chord from string 6 with (low to high) the middle, ring, index, and pinky fingers. Then, all you need to do to play the alternating bass is to pick the appropriate bass note in between the chordal double stops. For the A7 chords in measures 5–6 barre across all 6 strings at fret 5 and finger the chord (low to high) with the index, ring, pinky, middle, index and index.

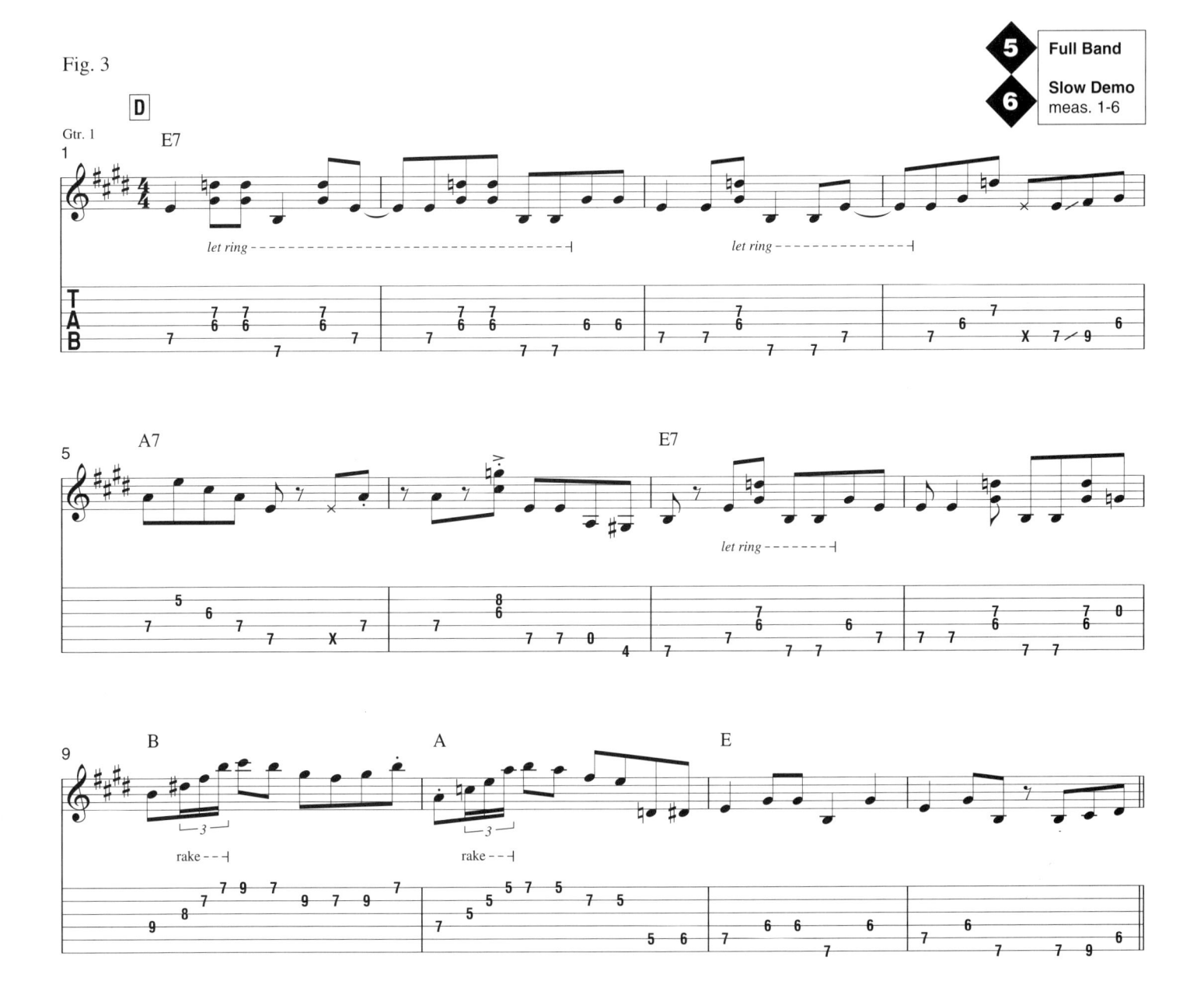

MR. MOTO

By Paul Johnson and Richard Delvy
Recorded by the Belairs in 1961

With a clean, lightly reverbed, minor key lead melody over a driving, eighth-note rhythm guitar, "Mr. Moto" (written by Paul Johnson when he was fourteen—the title refers to a Peter Lorre movie character) set down the template for the majority of music in the genre. By 1963 lead guitarist Eddie Bertrand and drummer Dick Delvy had split from rhythm guitarist Johnson, with Bertrand forming Eddie and the Showmen (later to include future session whiz Larry Carlton), and Delvy joining the Challengers. Johnson himself left the Belairs high and dry in 1964.

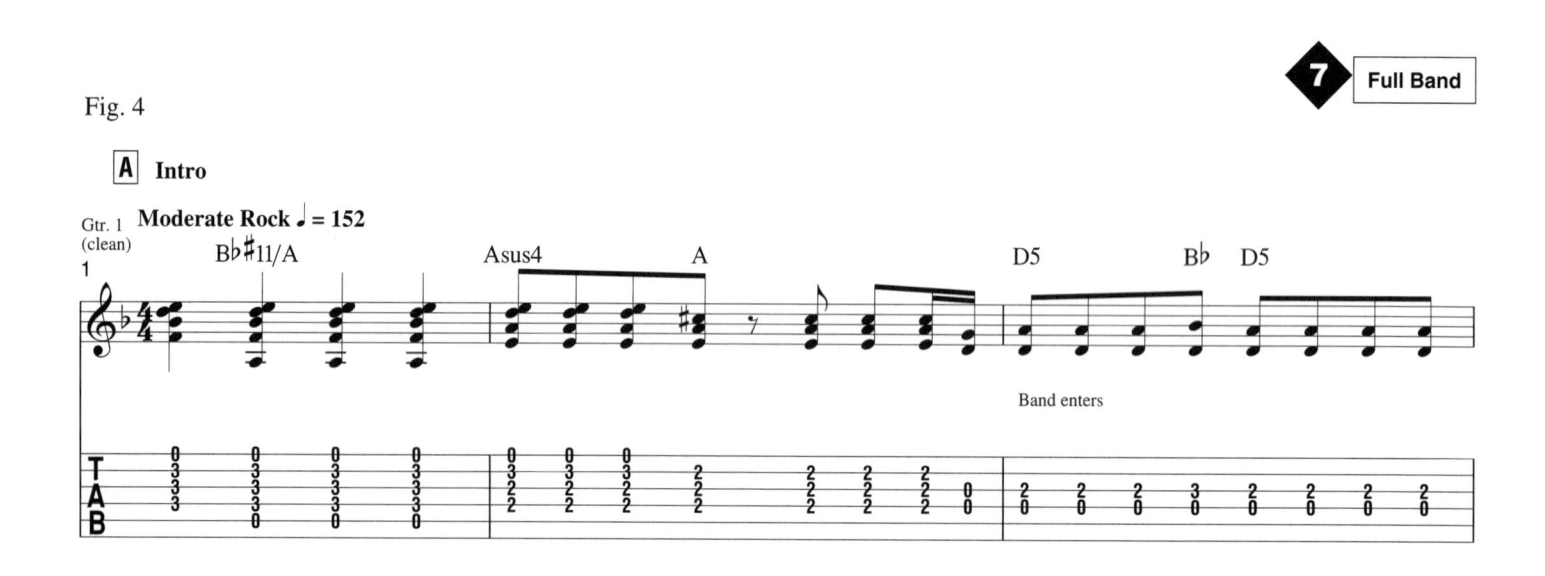

Figure 4 – Rehearsal Letter A (Intro)

The best surf instrumentals—indeed any popular instrumentals—sport catchy melodies and dynamic arrangements that hold the listener's attention even after repeated listening. "Mr. Moto" scores on all counts. The intro alone is a compositional gem, serving as a mini-overture that establishes the overall tonality and the eighth-note groove with just one guitar (Gtr. 1). Dig the "Spanish" vibe of the melancholy B♭♯11 voicing in measure 1 that creates instant anticipation. The Asus4 in measure 2 also contributes to this feeling that is partially resolved with the A major and then brought home harmonically with the D5 in measures 3 and 4 as the eight-note rhythm immediately turns the wick up.

Performance Tip: It is recommended that you play the broken D5 in measures 5 and 6 with alternating down and up pick strokes.

© 1961 and Renewed 1990 Miraleste Music Co.
All Rights Reserved

Figure 5 – Rehearsal Letter B

"Mr. Moto," like some other surf classics, is constructed on a foundation similar to the Ventures' "Walk Don't Run." Rehearsal Letters B and C repeat following two piano verses (Letter D, not shown, that changes keys to C) and a drum break, though the Belairs went the Ventures one better by returning to the intro to end the tune.

The eight measures of Letter B "shoot the curl" with i (Dm), ♭VI (B♭), V (A), and i changes, with each chord lasting two measures. Gtr. 1 (Johnson) segues smoothly from the intro with broken 5ths in pumping eighth notes relative to the D, B♭, A, and D (measure 7) chords before breaking into a strummed Dm triad in measure 8. Bertrand (Gtr. 2) combs the D Aeolian mode (a surfer fave) on the bass strings for his moody melody with two "note-worthy" exceptions. In measures 3 and 4 (♭VI) he adds the A♭ that functions as the ♭7th of B♭ for a bit of funky blues tonality.

Be aware that the notes from the D Aeolian mode (natural minor or relative minor of F major) have been skillfully manipulated in such a way that they also could be seen as the B♭ Mixolydian mode (especially in light of the ♭7th) in measures 3–4.

Performance Tip: For Gtr. 2, start each measure with the following fingers in order to access the other notes for each change in the most efficient manner: Measure 1—index, measure 3—middle, measure 5—ring, measure 6—middle, and measure 7—index.

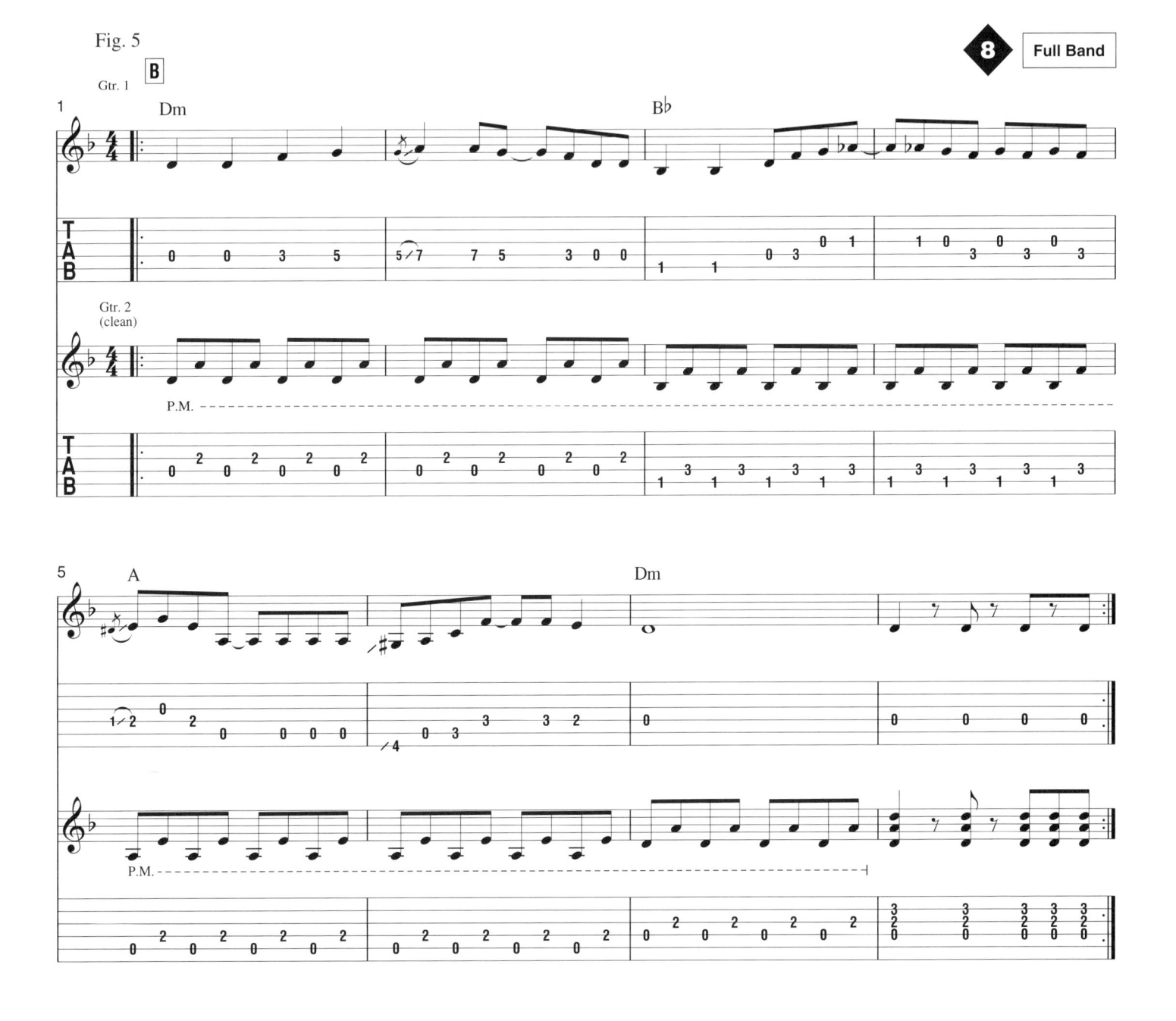

Figure 6 – Rehearsal Letter C

With the treble string melodies picked by Gtr. 1, and the major triads strummed by Gtr. 2, Letter C has a bright, buoyant quality that acts as a release from the somber, minor tonality of Letter B. Also eight measures long, it moves ♭VII (C), ♭VII, ♭III (F), ♭III, ♭VII, ♭VII, ♭III, and II (E). Dig that the rhythmic pattern played by Gtr. 2 appeared in 1950s rock 'n' roll, but became a common stylistic attribute of surf guitar in the early 1960s.

Gtr. 1 again follows the chord changes closely with carefully selected notes. For the ♭VII (C) chords in measures 1–2 and 5–6 he waxes the root (C), 2nd (D), 3rd (E), 4th (F), and 5th (G) notes. Cool, arpeggiated second-inversion (5th on bottom) F major triads (5th = C, root = F, and 3rd = A) serve the tight composition well in measures 3–4 and 7. For the II (E) chord in measure 8 Bertrand (Gtr. 1) applies the same relative triad (first strummed as a double stop with E/B = root and 5th on beats 1 and 2) as he employed for the ♭III (F), closing out the progression with a surprising whammy bar dip. (Note: Be hip that Letter C could be analyzed from the perspective of the relative minor key of Am with C = ♭III, F = ♭VI, and E = V. In that case, the scale played by Gtr. 1 would be the A Aeolian mode.)

Performance Tip: Form an open-position D major chord shape (low to high: index, ring, and middle fingers) for the F and E triads in measures 3, 4, 7, and 8.

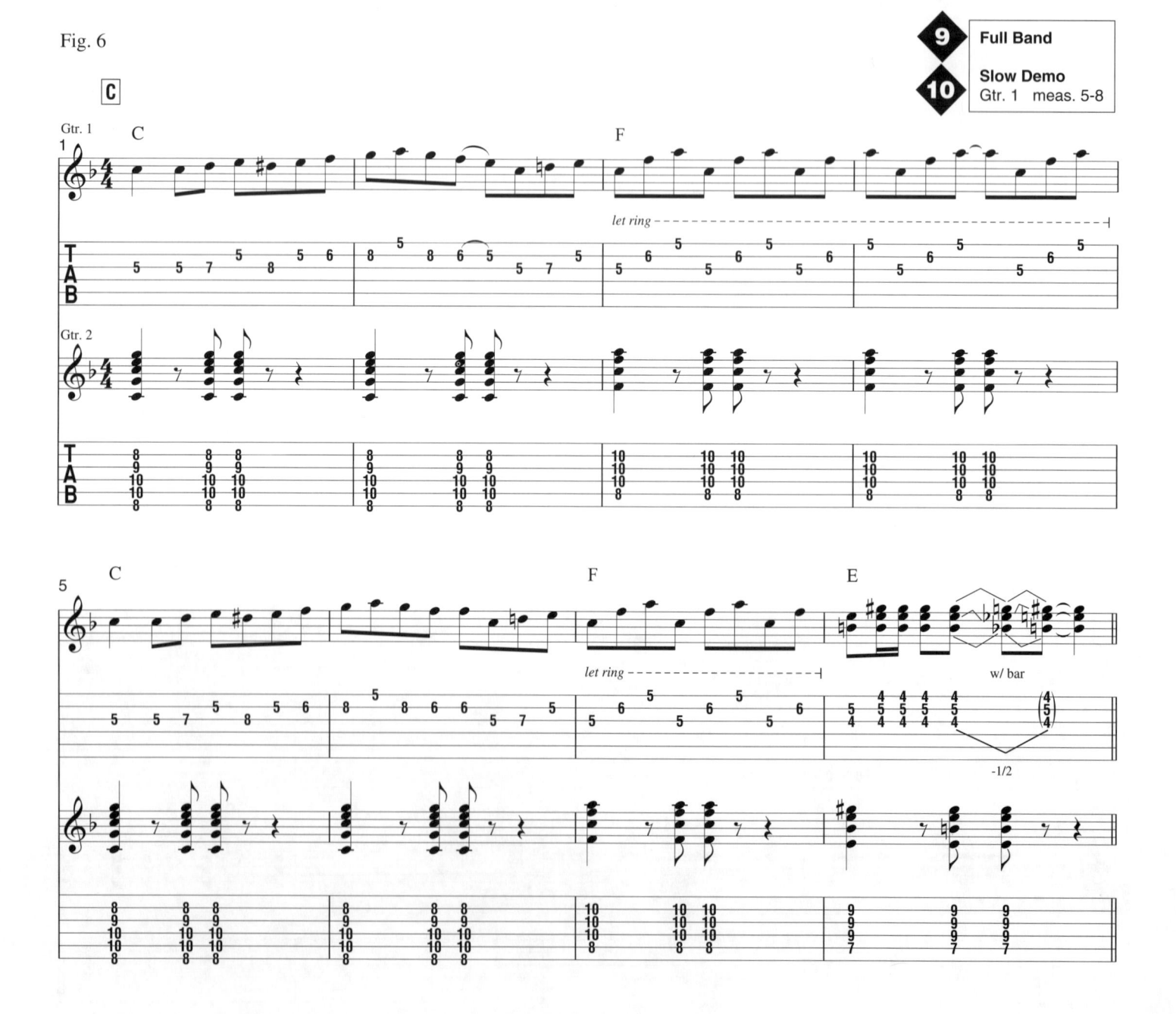

OUT OF LIMITS

By Michael Z. Gordon
Recorded by the Marketts in 1963

Like the Routers and other instrumental groups cobbled together to capitalize on the instrumental/surf music craze in the early 1960s, the Marketts were a band of Los Angeles session cats that included guitarist Tommy Tedesco, pianist Leon Russell, and drummer Jim Gordon. Organized by producer Joe Saraceno, who had worked with the Ventures, they had made a previous run at the charts with the pioneering, if lightweight, "Surfer's Stomp" (#31) in 1962 and then had an "out of sight" hit at #3 in early 1964 with "Out of Limits." A catchy ditty based on *The Twilight Zone* TV show theme, named for another sci-fi show, *Outer Limits*, and astonishingly similar to "Telstar" in the bridge (Rehearsal Letter C), it was ironically one of the last "surf" singles of note.

Figure 7 – Rehearsal Letter A (Intro)

Letter A functions as an intro and consists of twelve measures, though it is decidedly not a blues! Measure 1 (with a repeat) finds Gtr. 1 stating the main theme beamed up from the E minor pentatonic scale with the crucial addition of the dissonant ♭4th: A♭ (or major 3: G♯). Dig that this "spooky" little riff is lifted whole from the *Twilight Zone* theme song. Following is a 4-measure phrase of vi (Em), I (G), II (A) and III (B) that bears a striking relationship to the verse of the Yardbirds' "For Your Love" (1965).

As Gtr. 2 strums partial barre chords in whole notes (in slash notation), Gtr. 1 repeats the riff (E, G, A♭ and G) over each chord with the notes functioning as the root, ♭3rd, major 3rd and ♭3rd (Em), the 6th, root, ♭2nd and root (G), the 5th, ♭7th, major 7th and ♭7th (A). For the B chord, however, the A♭ is raised to A (♭7th), with the notes functioning as the 4th, ♭6th, ♭7th, and ♭6th.

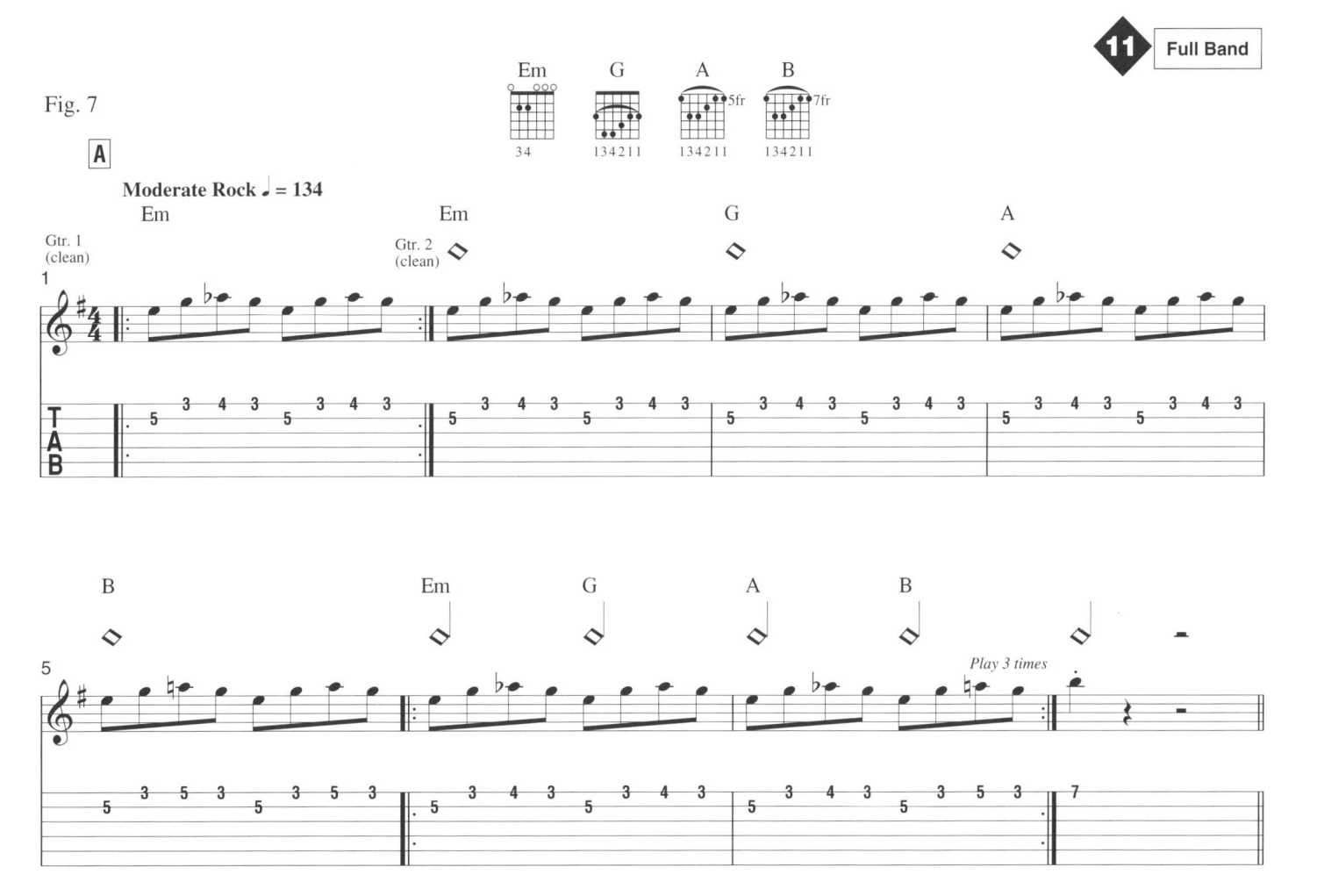

© 1963 (Renewed 1991) GOJO MUSIC (BMI) and MARATHON MUSIC (BMI)/ Administered by BUG MUSIC
All Rights Reserved   Used by Permission

Figure 8 – Rehearsal Letter B

In Rehearsal Letter B measure 1 repeats measure 1 of Rehearsal Letter A with Gtr. 1 again playing the riff unaccompanied. Measures 2 and 3 then repeat the four-chord, two-measure part as played by Gtr. 2 in measures 5–6 of Letter A. Gtr. 1, however, drops an octave and introduces the second theme at this point in time (or "out of time"!). Simple but so catchy that it sticks in the mind like a subliminal alien message, it uses the root (E), ♭3rd (G), 4th (A), and hip ♭5th (B♭, bent up a half step from the A) notes from the E blues scale at the fifth position. Note the cool double-picking at measure 4. Gtr. 2 contributes to the propulsion of this section by igniting the night with a driving, syncopated strum for each chord that continues with a slight variation in the next six measures.

Measures 6–12 are actually an exact repeat, harmonically, of measures 2–5 with Gtr. 1 using his booster rockets to achieve orbit (an octave higher) with yet a third theme in measures 7–9. Phrased similarly to the second theme, it uses the root (E), ♭7th (D), and dissonant ♭2nd (F, bent up a half step from E) to build altitude as this pop masterpiece soars into outer space. Measures 10 and 11 then complete the logic of the composition by repeating the G and B changes of measures 4 and 5.

Performance Tip: If you approach every riff and lick, including the triads in measures 4–5 and 10–11, by starting with your ring finger (or placing it on the lowest string for the triads), it should be obvious how to finger what follows.

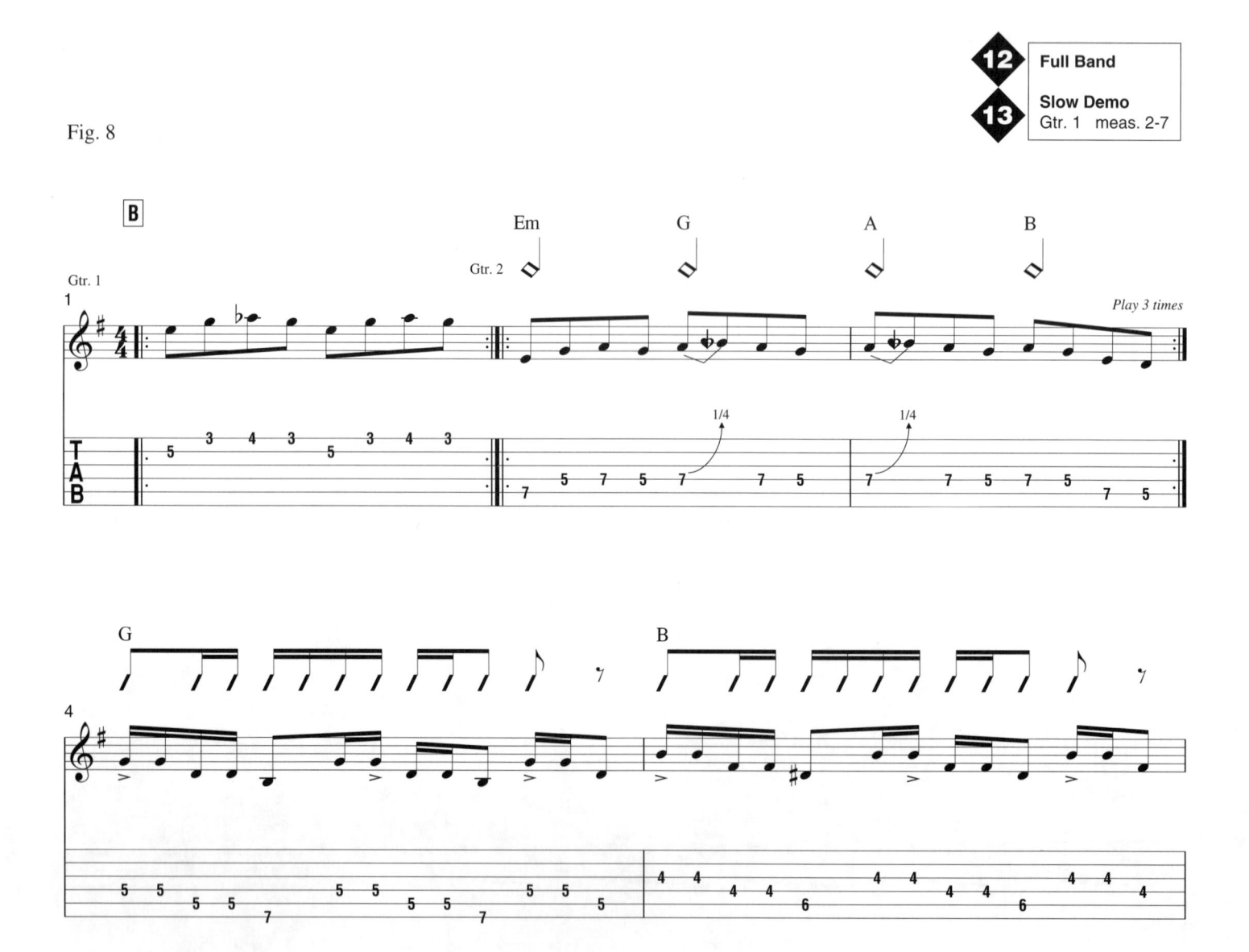

Fig. 8

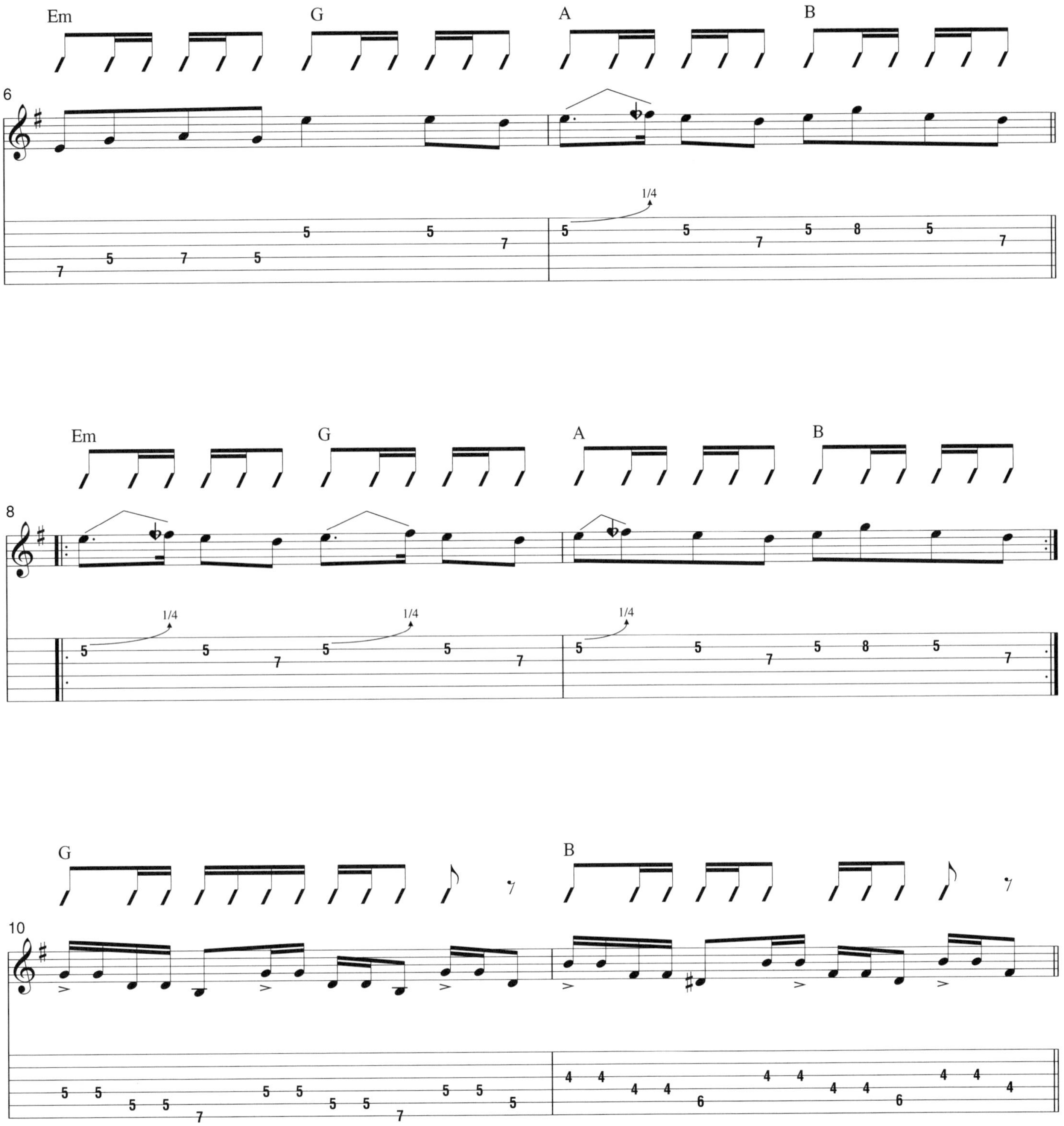
Em
G
A
B
6
1/4
Em
G
A
B
8
1/4
1/4
1/4
G
B
10

PENETRATION
By Steven Leonard
Recorded by the Pyramids in 1963

Either hailed as brilliant primitivists or reviled as no-talent opportunists, the Pyramids, from Long Beach, California, are rightly acknowledged as one of the last bona fide surf bands to surface from the genre. They had their one hit (#18) in 1964 with "Penetration." Bassist Steve Leonard penned the tune in direct homage to "Pipeline," creating another surf masterpiece in its own right.

Figure 9 – Rehearsal Letter A

Following three measures of drums, rhythm guitar (Gtr. 2), and bass up front, Rehearsal Letters A and B present 20-measure verses based on blues changes. The most obvious nod to "Pipeline" occurs in the surging, "penetrating" bass line. Employing the root, 5th, and ♭7th notes of the i (F#m) and iv (Bm), it provides exceptional forward motion.

Leonard's approach to writing the melody prompted him to pen a descending minor key line as opposed to the ascending one of "Pipeline." There's nuthin' fancy here—just straight F# and B minor pentatonic tones in the keys of F#m and Bm and exactly the same relative to each chord change. The use of subtle whammy bar action on the root notes in measures 6, 10, and 14 provides the perfect accent, "bending" the time dynamically against the waves of eighth notes that flow through "Penetration." Check out the Ventures' "Walk Don't Run" and almost anything by Chet Atkins to hear a similar artistic approach with the bar.

Performance Tip: Access the bass pattern with the ring and index fingers and use alternate picking for efficiency.

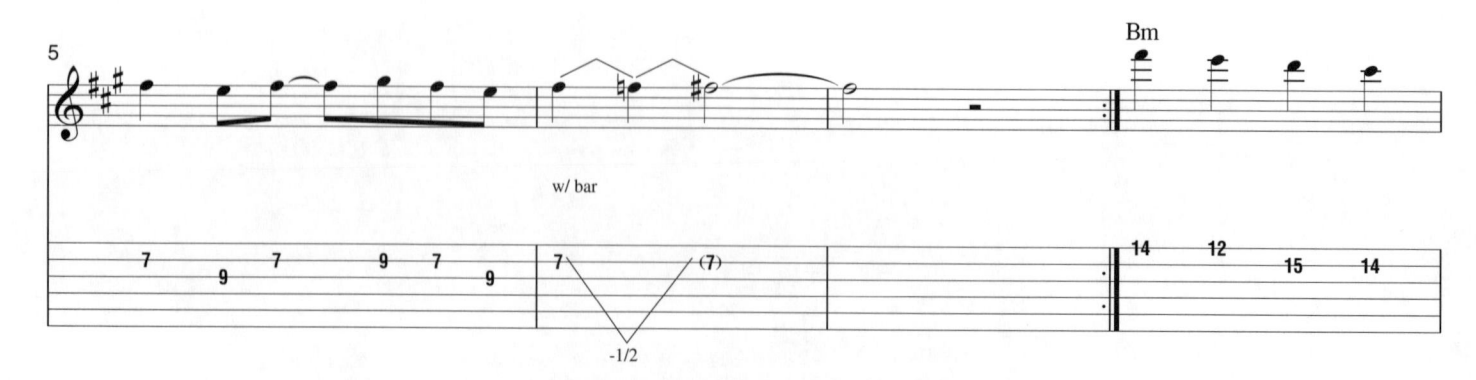

© 1964 (Renewed 2001) Winston Music Publishers (ASCAP)
All Rights Reserved   Used by Permission

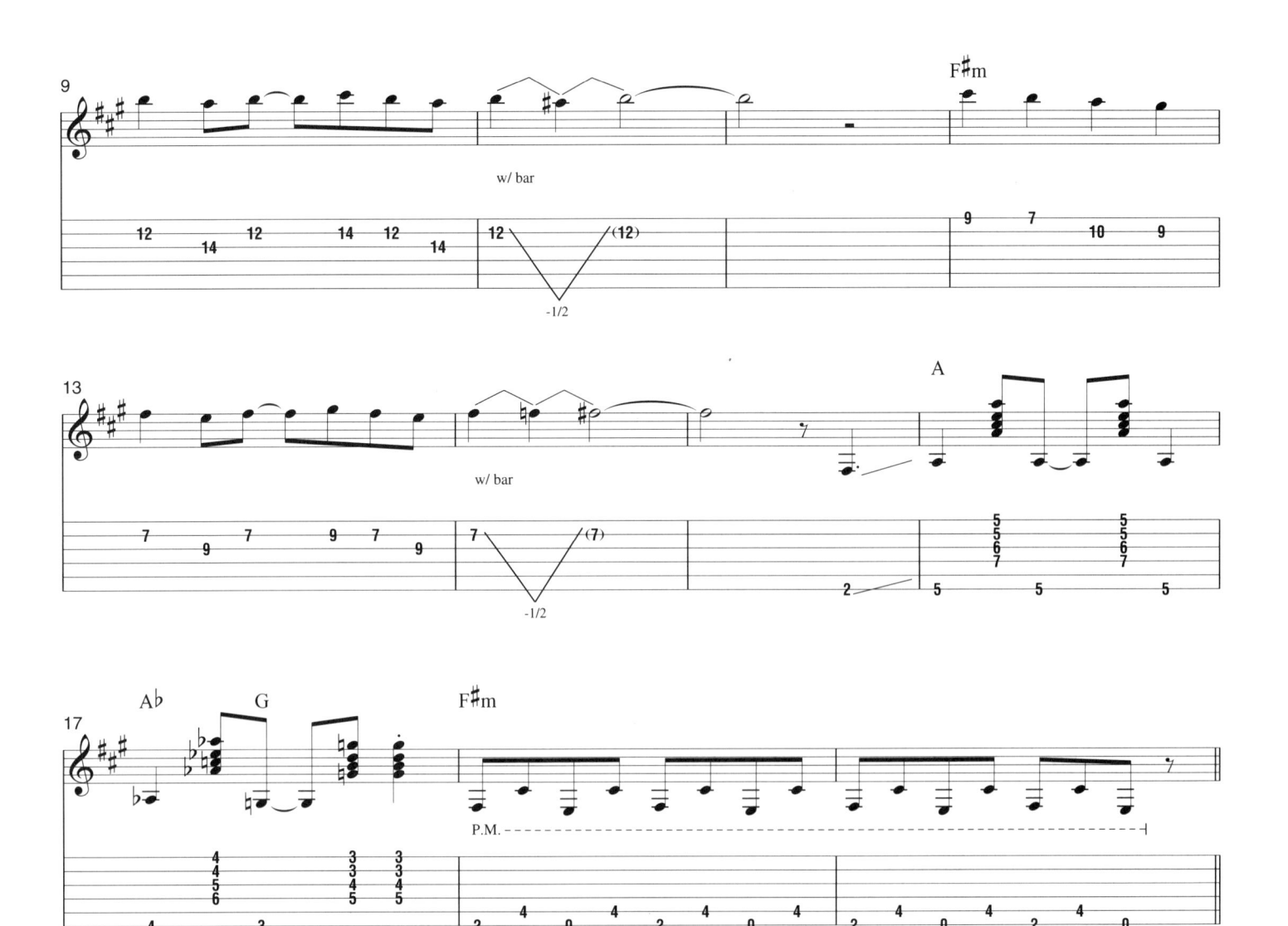

Figure 10 – Rehearsal Letter B

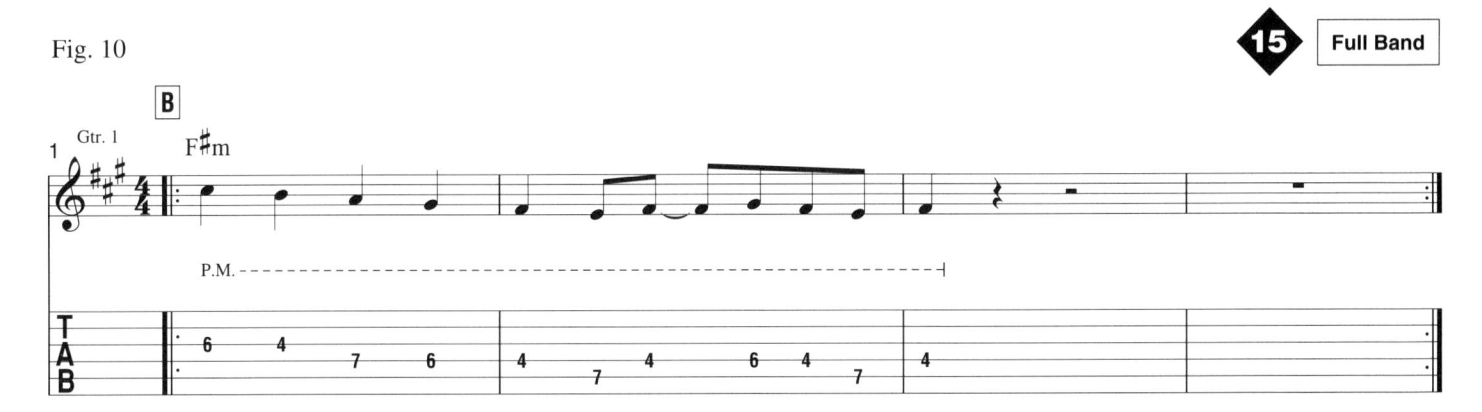

Rehearsal Letter B is a virtual repeat of Letter A, but with the melody played one octave lower. A simple solution to the compositional problem of how to add interest and variety without creating an entirely new part, perhaps, but it works due to the quiet strength of the melody. Dig the palm muting in measures 1–16 that, besides variety, adds drama, dynamics, and a slight air of mystery.

Performance Tip: Lay the edge of your right-hand (pick hand) palm, below the pinky, across the bridge of your axe to mute the strings while applying more wrist action than usual to spank the notes with the pick.

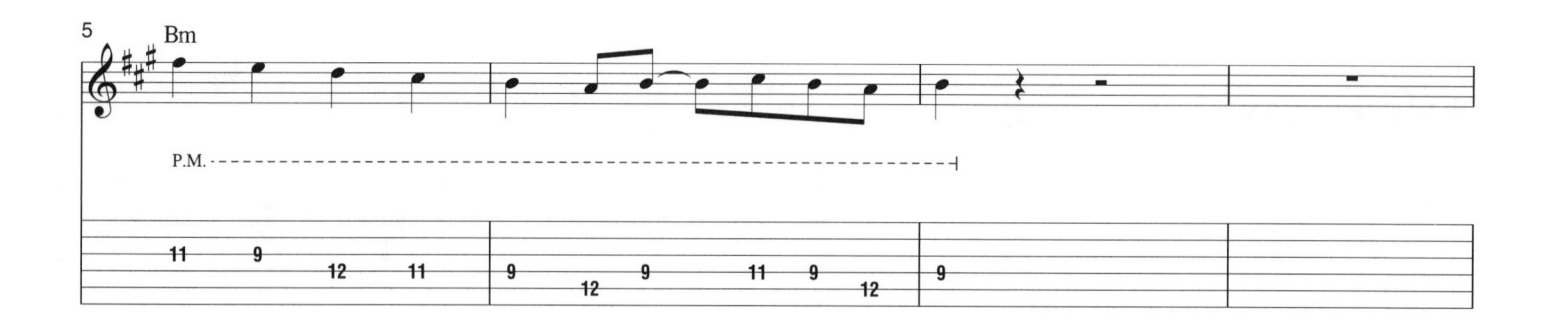

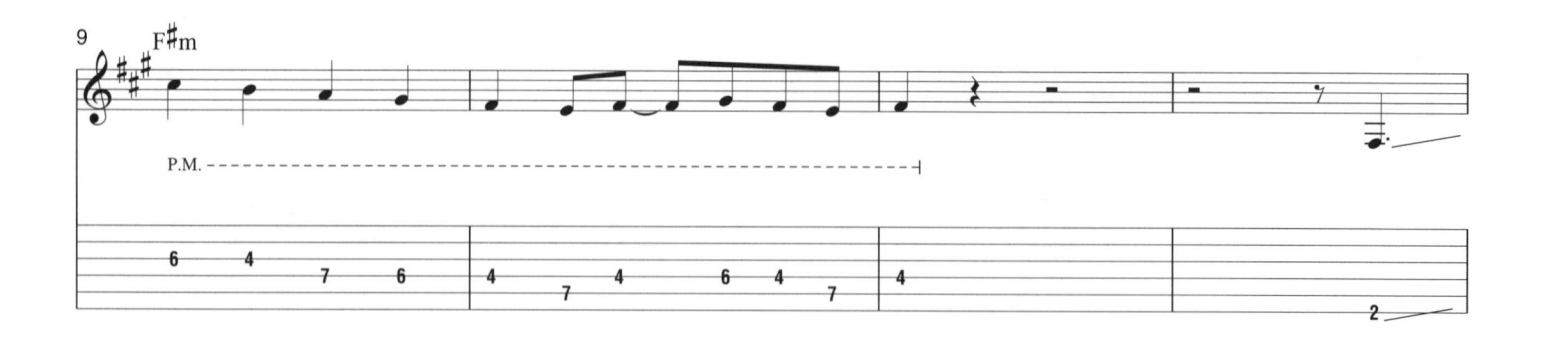

Figure 11 – Rehearsal Letter C

Functioning as a bridge or release from the "verses" of Letters A and B, Rehearsal Letter C takes "Penetration" to a whole new place. A good analogy would be coming into the bright sunshine or up on the sand after a (blonde) hair-raising ride through the shadow of the curl. The sixteen measures use a combination of chords diatonic to A major (save for G, the ♭VII), except that chords which are usually minor in this key (ii: Bm, and vi: F#m) are major in this progression.

The arrangement is hardly brain surgery, with the guitar simply arpeggiating triads over the muted root-note pulse of the backup. The effect, however, is right on the money, with a section that contrasts the subdued, minor key tonality of Letters A and B. Contributing mightily to the power of the composition is the fact that Rehearsal Letter D (not shown), the last section of "Penetration," is the same as Letters A and B, except that now the melody is transposed up an octave above that of Letter A. Following Letter C, it makes for an uplifting experience and satisfying conclusion for all!

Performance Tip: Use the following fingerings for the triads: B—barre with index, A—(low to high) ring, middle, and index, G—(low to high) middle and index as a barre, F#—(low to high) index, ring, and middle.

18

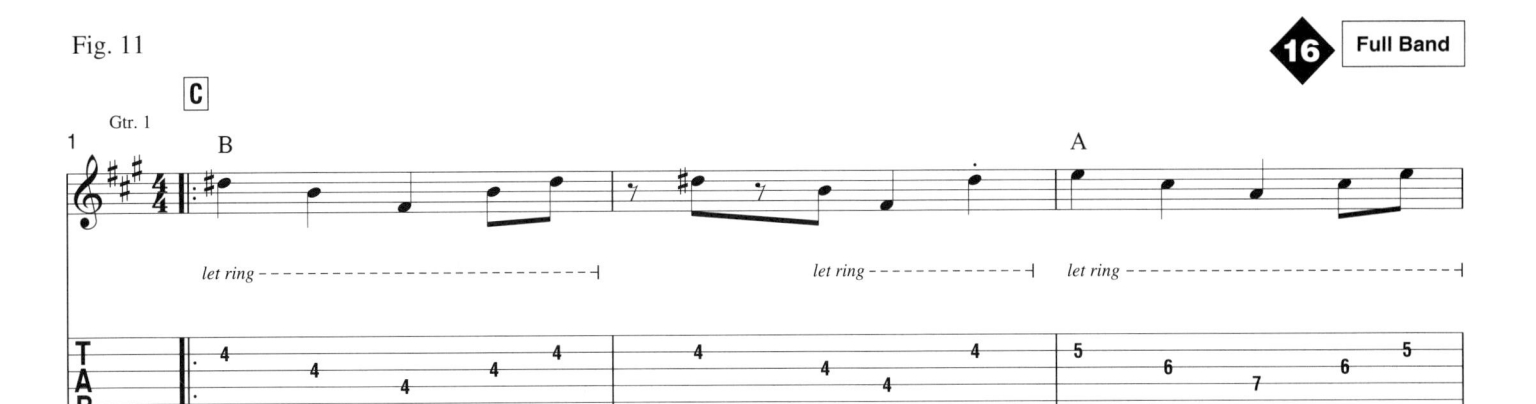

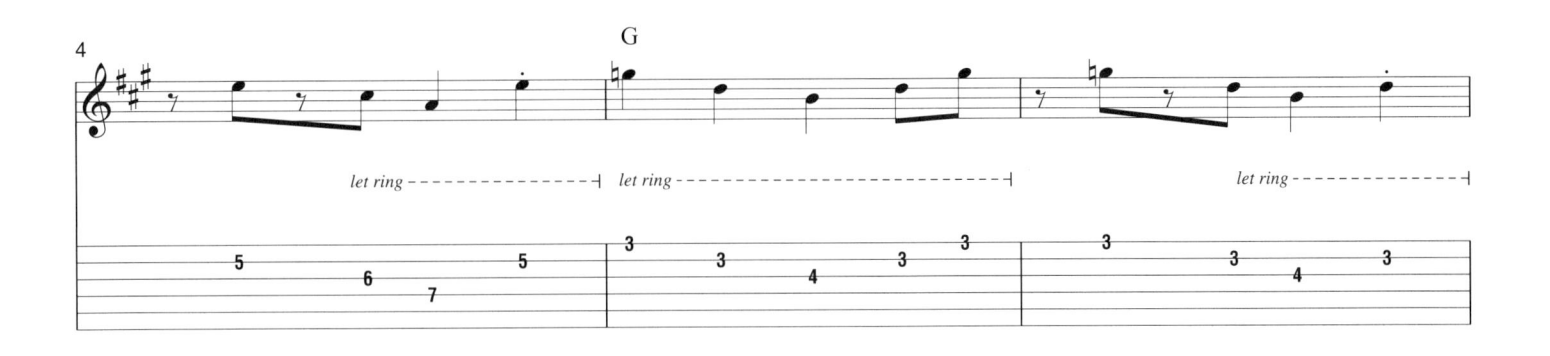

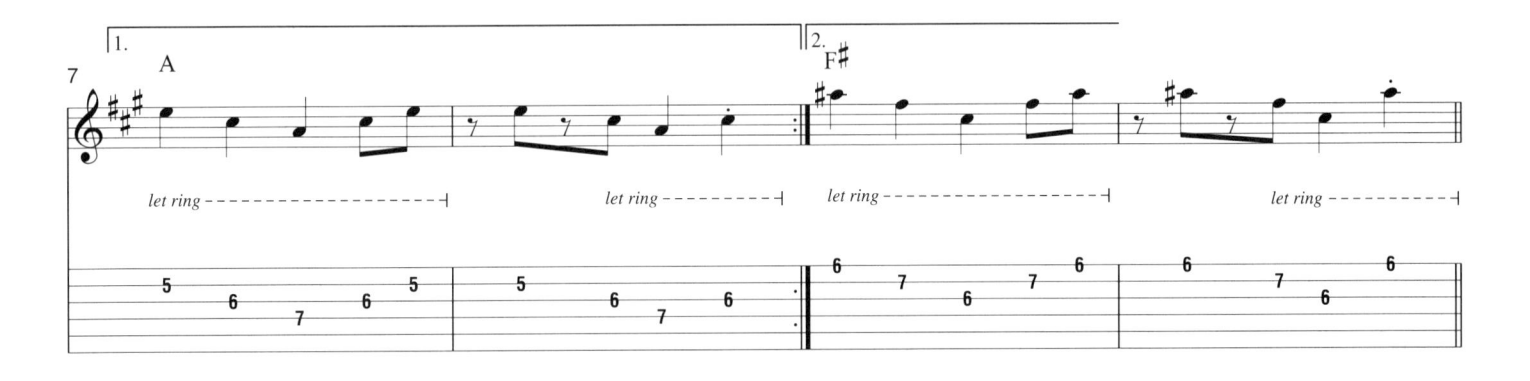

PIPELINE

By Bob Spickard and Brian Carman
Recorded by the Chantays in 1963

The Chantays could be classified as "one-hit wonders," perhaps, but what a hit! Originally recorded for Downey Records in December of 1962, it was reissued on Dot Records in January of 1963 and promptly "hung ten" to #4 on the pop charts. It was then re-released in 1966 and still made a respectable showing at #106, though the surf era was virtually wiped out. Everything from the watery reverb and dense, muted mix to the minor key licks paints an atmospheric, aural picture evocative of the surf, sand, and sun that will stand the test of time as a classic.

Figure 12 – Rehearsal Letter B (Theme)

Following Rehearsal Letter A (Intro – not shown) with its signature glissando down string 5, and eight measures of the Em bass pattern played by Gtr. 1, a creative, twenty-two-measure verse ensues. Though essentially based on i (Em)–iv (Am)–V (B) blues changes (with the ♭VI, C, thrown in), the progression deviates from standard 12-, 8-, or 16-bar blues forms.

In measures 1–4 (Em) Gtr. 1 (Carman) plays a pulsing, hypnotic unison line with the bass utilizing the root (E), 5th (B), and ♭3rd (G) notes. In measures 5–8 (Am) he picks the same pattern relative to the key of A (A, E, and C notes). He then ramps up the rhythm in measures 9–15 with pounding sixteenth notes of just the root of each chord change.

Gtr. 2 (Spickard) creates an elegantly simple but timeless melody in measures 1–8 from the E minor hexatonic and A minor hexatonic scales, respectively.

Performance Tip: Dig that Gtr. 1 plays his parts palm-muted throughout. For the glissando in measure 16 you must apply just enough pressure to hear pitch, but not so much that you hear *individual* pitches at each fret as you steadily glide your index finger down string 5.

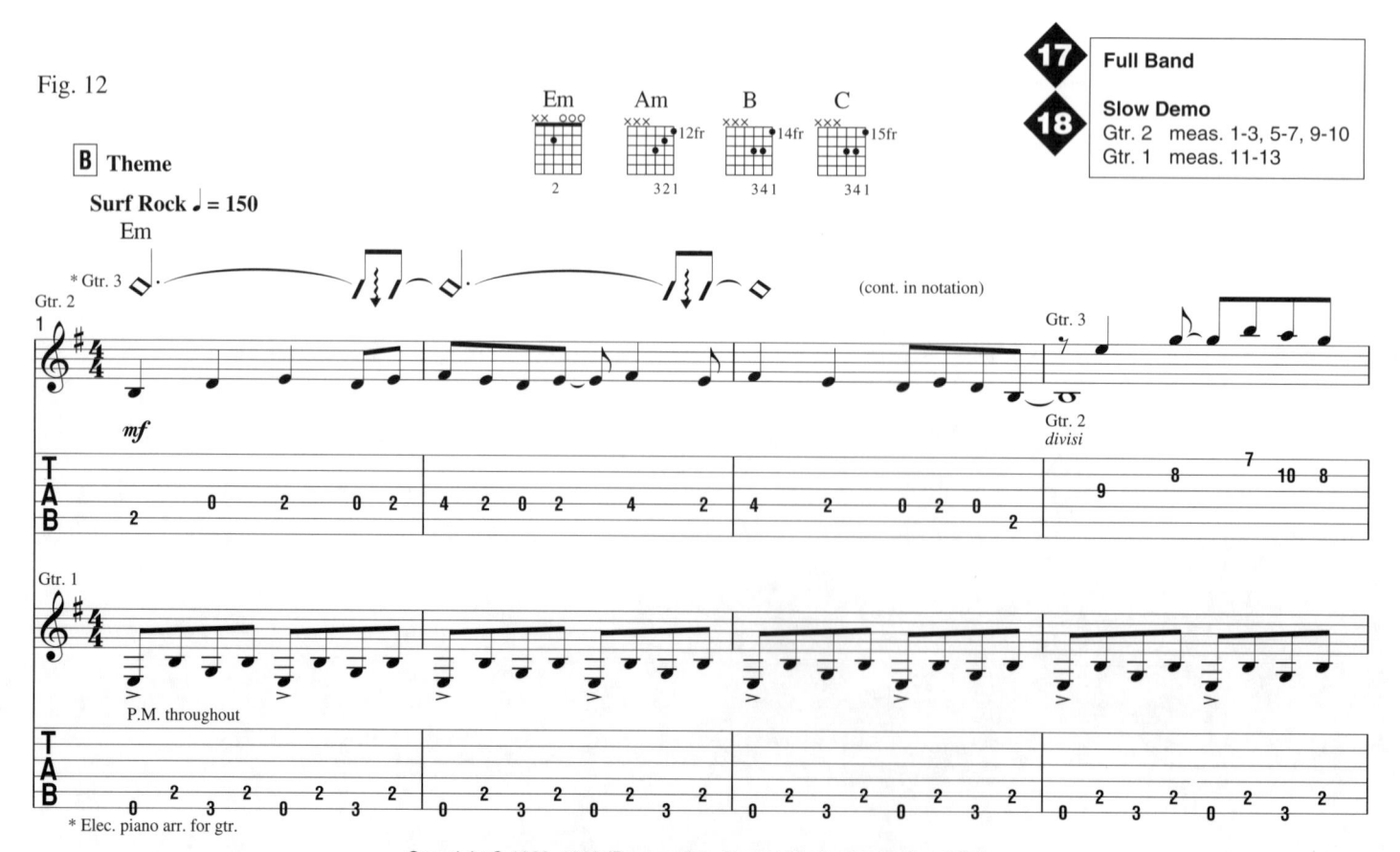

Copyright © 1962, 1963 (Renewed) by Regent Music Corporation (BMI)
International Copyright Secured   All Rights Reserved
Used by Permission

Am
Gtr. 3
(Gtr. 3 cont. in notation)
Gtr. 3
5
(Gtr. 3 cont. in slash)
Gtr. 2
divisi
(Gtr. 3 cont. in slash)
B
C
B
Gtr. 3
9
Gtr. 2
Gtr. 1
C
B
12

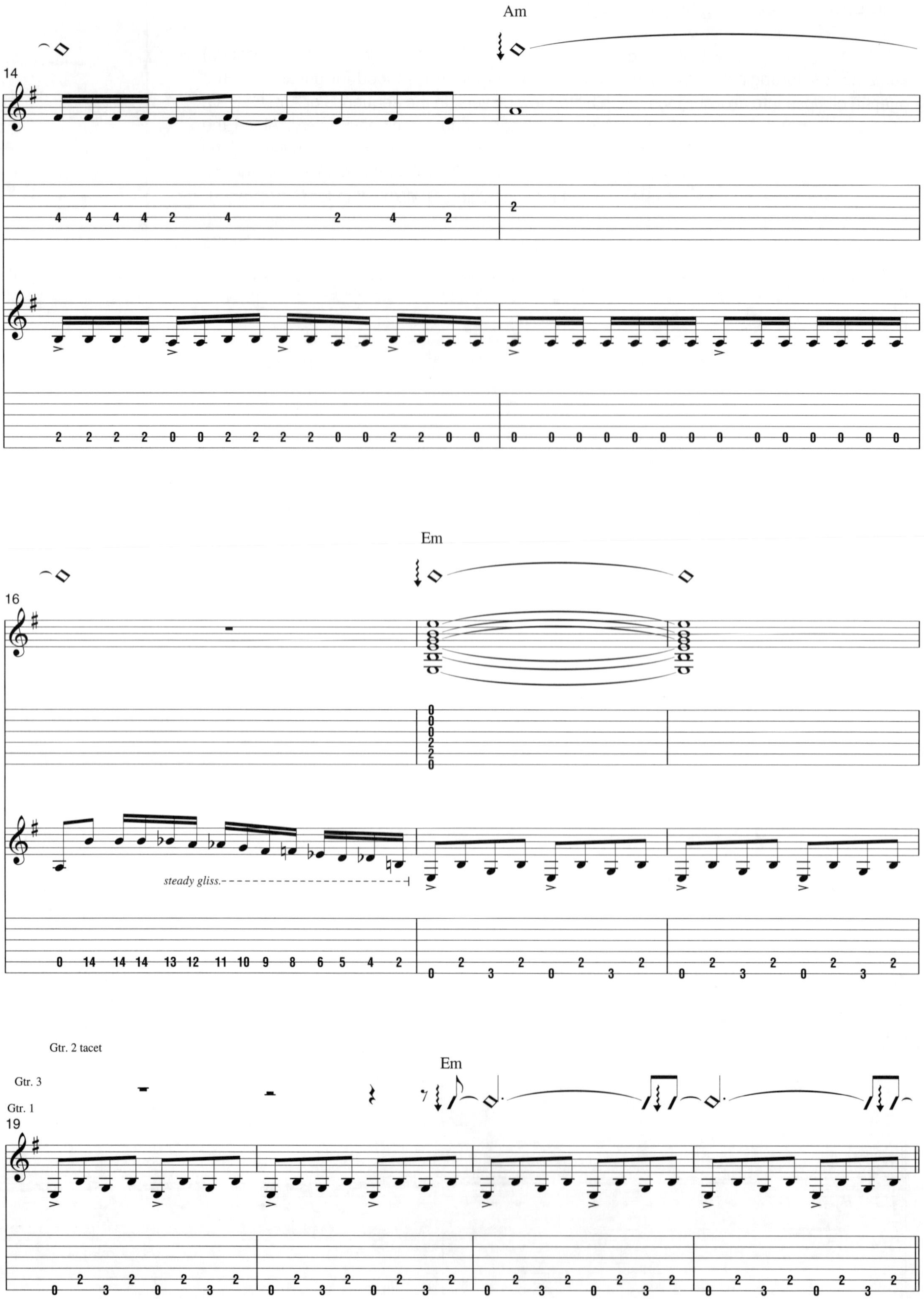
Am
14
Em
16
steady gliss.
Gtr. 2 tacet
Gtr. 3
Gtr. 1
Em
19

Figure 13 – Rehearsal Letter C (Bridge)

The sixteen-measure bridge (comprised of two similar eight-measure sections) contains a solo originally played by piano man Marshall. Transcribed for guitar (Gtr. 3) it offers a glimpse into an approach taken by too few players. In the sequence of Am–G–F–G, based on a classic flamenco progression (and appearing prominently in "All Along the Watchtower" and the solo to "Stairway to Heaven") each change receives a similar melody based around its chord tones. All are derived from the A natural minor scale, producing the correct mode for each diatonic chord in A minor, including G Mixolydian for G (VII) and F Lydian for F (VI). Though the triadic tones (root, 3rd and 5th) are highlighted for each chord, each pattern is phrased slightly differently. In addition, the 2nd (B and A) is included for the Am and G, respectively, while the F pattern includes the #4th (B) note. Observe that measures 15 and 16 resolve to the v (Em) chord with ascending and descending arpeggios at fret 12.

Gtr. 1 keeps the waters churning and boiling with bass string sixteenth notes involving the root notes of the chord changes, similar to measures 9–15 of the Theme (Letter B), except for measure 16 where he repeats the famous glissando.

Performance Tip: When you realize that Gtr. 3 plays out of chord shapes for each change, you can position your fingers accordingly for the utmost efficiency. For the Am and F chords use the ring finger for the lowest note (root) and then apply the middle and index fingers above for the other notes. For the G chord, barre across strings 3 and 2 at fret 12 with the index finger and then use the pinky and ring fingers as necessary. For the Em chord place the ring finger at fret 14 on string 4 and then barre strings 3, 2, and 1 with the index finger, adding the second finger on the second string at the thirteenth fret for the addition of the C in the piano melody.

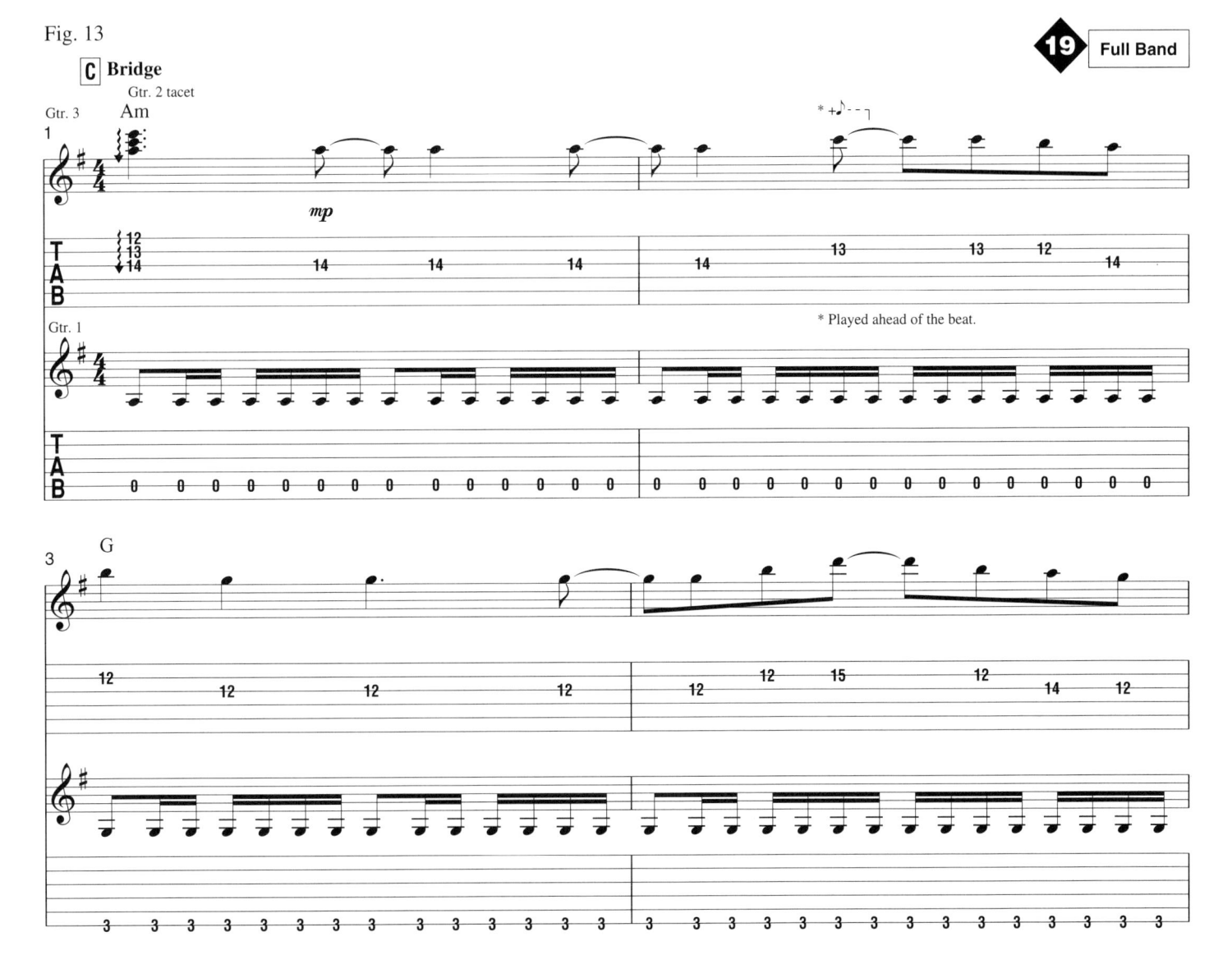

*Played ahead of the beat.

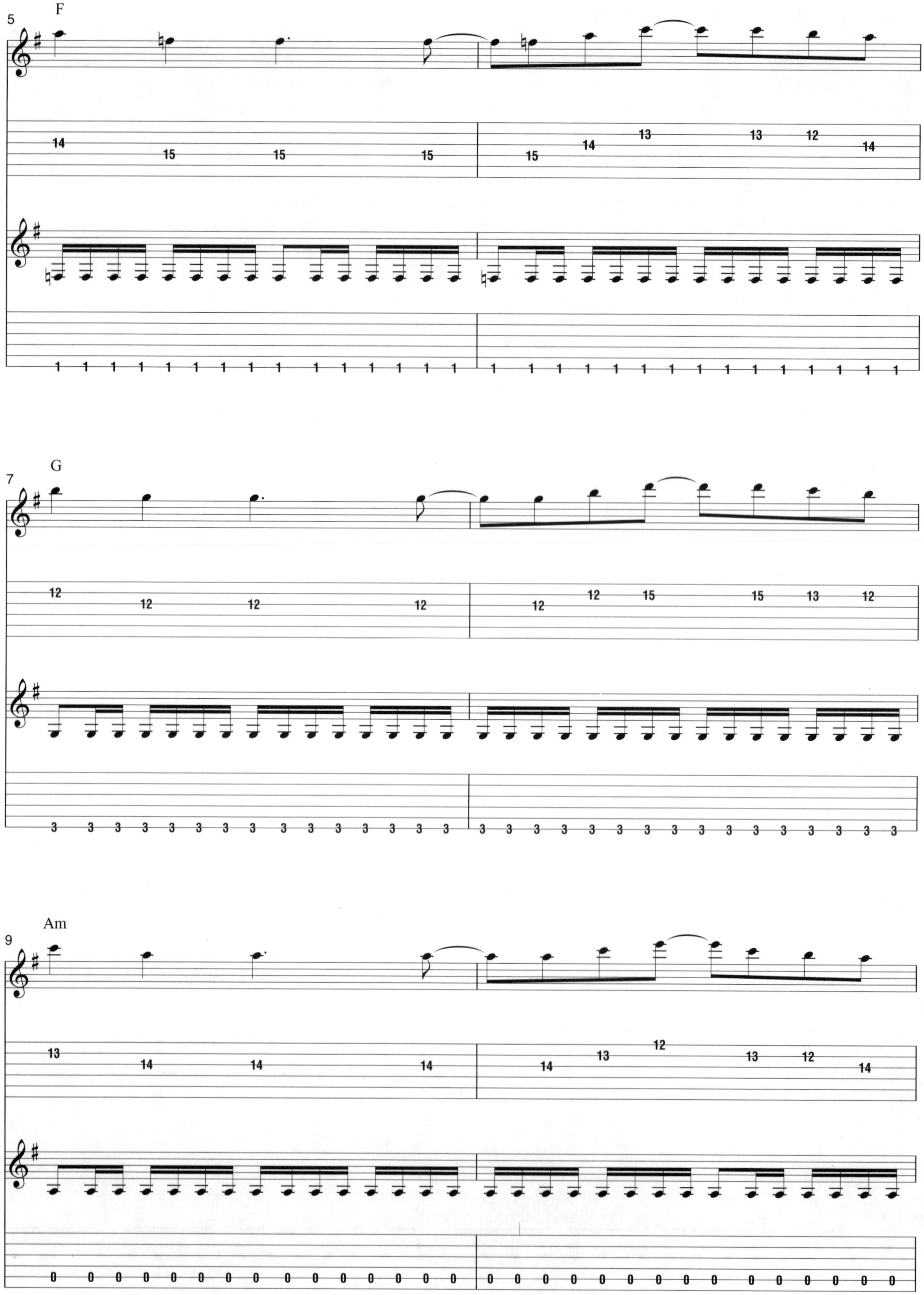
5
F
7
G
9
Am

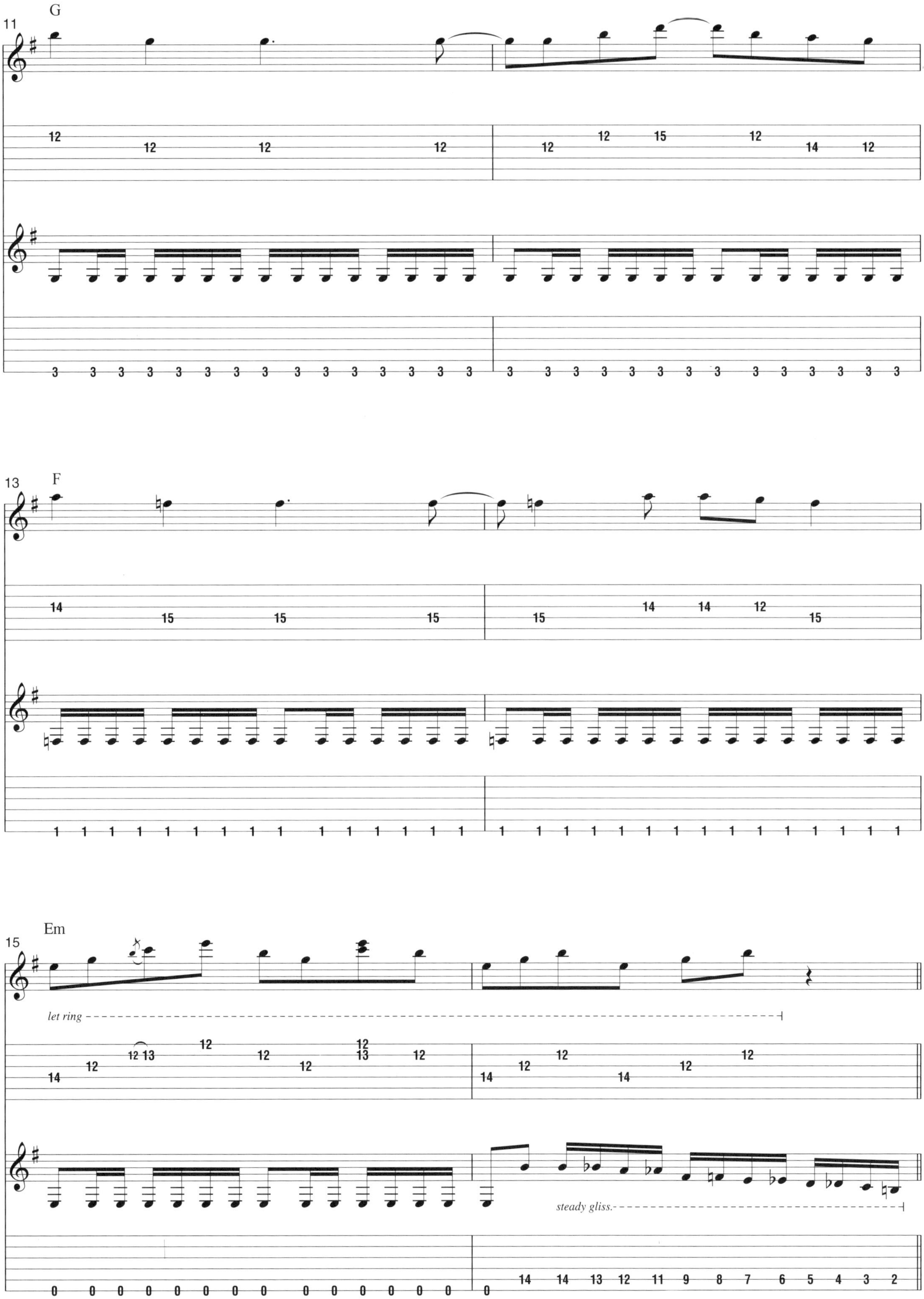
11
G
13
F
15
Em
let ring
steady gliss.

SHAKE 'N' STOMP

By Dick Dale
Recorded by Dick Dale and the Del-Tones in 1962

"Shake 'n' Stomp" was Dick Dale's follow-up single in March of 1962 to "Let's Go Trippin'," one of his 12-bar blues arrangements his fans had originally referred to as "The Stomp." When the crushing "Miserlou" followed two months later the Dick Dale legend was cast in stone, but the crucial elements of the genre had already been defined by the master.

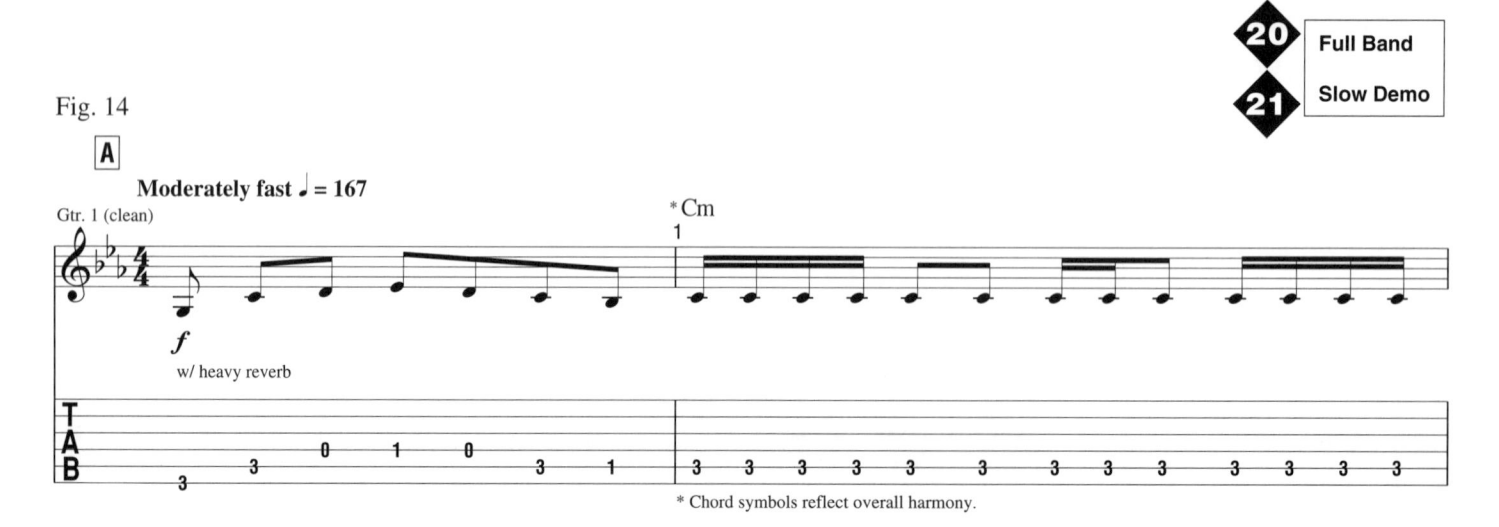

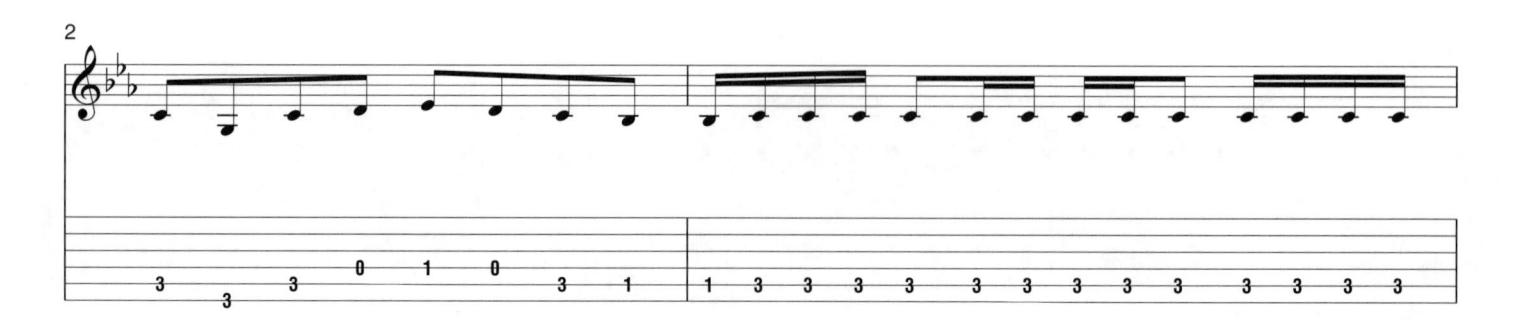

Figure 14 – Rehearsal Letter A

Like so much other great surf music, "Shake 'n' Stomp" is a 12-bar minor blues progression with a dominant seventh chord for the V. Similar to "Let's Go Trippin'," every other measure contains a hip arpeggio-type bass run relative to the chord (the pickup and measures 2 and 8) or in anticipation of the upcoming change (measures 4, 6, and 10) when it occurs in the measure preceding the new chord. Dig, however, that Dale did not compose this little gem quite that programmatically. The bass pattern in measure 8 (i) that precedes the V, as well as the pattern in measure 10 (V), is essentially the same phrasing with exactly the same notes.

Closer inspection reveals what Dale was up to in this clever arrangement. The notes G, C, D, E♭, and B♭, while diatonic to the key signature of C minor, also function as the root, 4th, 5th, ♭6th, and bluesy sharp 9th (A♯) of the G7 (V7) chord. Most likely, however, Dale heard the pattern as related to the Cm change only, as it occurs in measure 8 (i) and measure 10 (V preceding the i). Whatever the theory involved, the result is a subtle adjustment that keeps the tune from sounding so predictable as it flies through the changes. Also of interest is the use of the raised sixth (A♮) in measure 11, a hint of the C Dorian mode.

20 Full Band
21 Slow Demo

Fig. 14

A

Moderately fast ♩ = 167

Gtr. 1 (clean)

Cm

f
w/ heavy reverb

* Chord symbols reflect overall harmony.

Copyright © 1961 Surf Beat Music (ASCAP)
Copyright Renewed
All Rights Reserved   Used by Permission

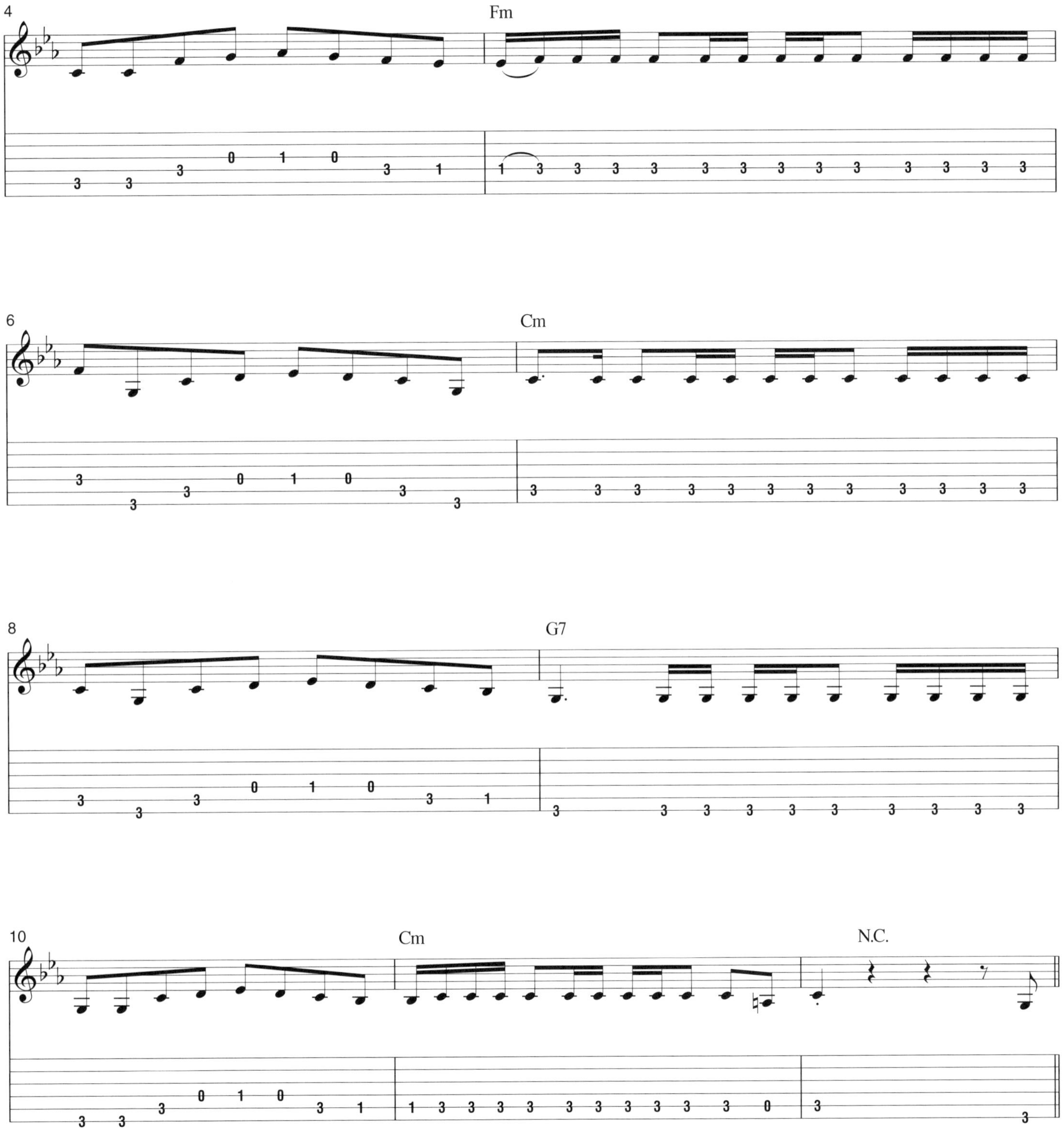
4
Fm
6
Cm
8
G7
10
Cm
N.C.

Figure 15 – Rehearsal Letter B

Dick Dale takes the blues and filters it through his unique view of soloing "surf guitar style" in Rehearsal Letter B by sticking close to the key target notes of the changes. Though he does not create "wave after wave" of tension and release as a great blues artist would, he nonetheless alludes to the practice. Using the C blues scale in eighth position (with the addition of the hip 6th, A, in measure 1) like a musical surfboard, he maintains his balance by keeping the eighth and sixteenth notes in the "pipeline" with controlled fury. Dig the cool blues bends to the tonality-defining ♭3rd (E♭) in measure 1 from the 2nd (D) that set the tone for his 12-bar ride. By measures 3 and 4 (i) he has settled in to "stomping" away on the root (C) with the occasional inclusion of the bluesy ♭7th (B♭) note.

In measures 5 and 6 over the iv chord (Fm) he likewise sticks on the root note (F), though he cannot resist the stone blues half-step bend from the root (F) to the ♭2nd (G♭). Similar to measures 1–4, the root note (C) becomes the object of his attention once again in measures 7–8 (i), though he does anticipate the upcoming V (G7) chord in measure 9 by playing the ♭3rd and 4th on beat 4 of measure 8. Notice how Dale acknowledges the V chord tonality with the ♭7th (F) along with the tension-producing bend from the ♭7th to the unusual major 7th (G♭ or F♯). In measure 10 (iv) he plays almost the same pattern of notes, with the F, G♭, E♭, C, and B♭ notes now functioning as the root, ♭2nd, ♭7th, 5th, and 4th—rich melodic choices. No surprises in measure 11 over the i as he slaps the root (C) note around before resting in the stop-time of measure 12.

Performance Tip: As with all of Dale's music, it is necessary to use the strength of your forearm by picking from the elbow, rather than the wrist, to execute the fast strumming.

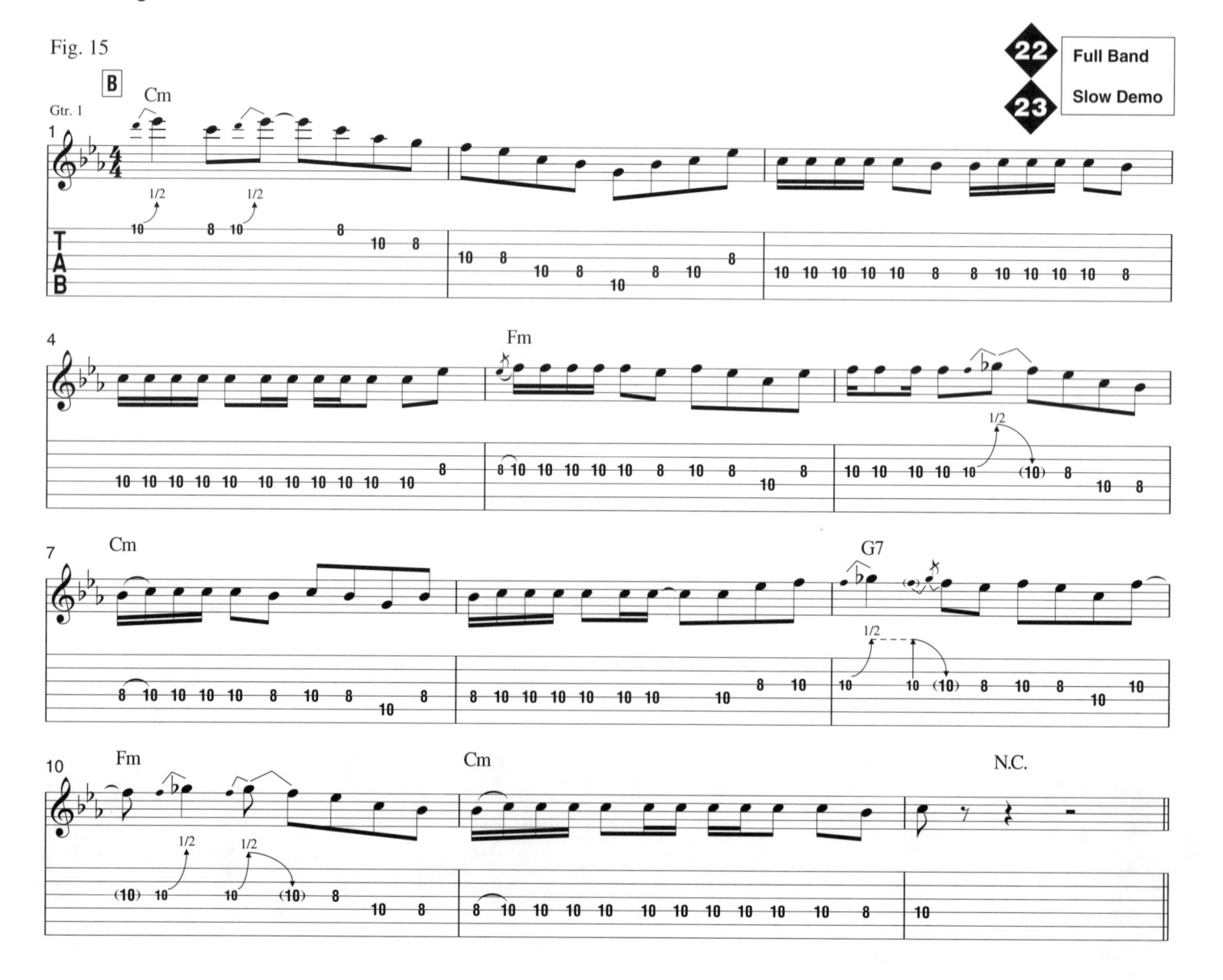

Figure 16 – Rehearsal Letter E

Dale shows his inventiveness in Rehearsal Letter E when he changes registers upward by an octave and pummels the root notes for twelve measures in a variation on the main theme of Rehearsal Letter A. Subtleties and musical surprises abound, however. In measures 1–4 (Cm) he includes the ♭3rd (E♭) once, along with the root (C) and ♭7th (B♭) notes. He inserts a slinky bend of the root (F) to the ♭2nd (G♭) in measure 6 over the iv chord (Fm) followed by the ♭7th (E♭), 5th (C), and 4th (B♭). Check out how the B♭ anticipates the same note on beat 1 of measure 7 over the i chord.

Measure 8 (i) starts to substantially deviate from the drill as Dale plays octave root notes (C) while ending the measure with the dynamic texture and "improved" harmony of the C/G (root/5th) and B♭/F (♭7th/4th) dyads. He ratchets up the energy one last time in measure 9 (V) chord with the rat-a-tat of the root (G) note. Observe the smart inclusion of the G♭ passing tone on beat 4, however, that leads down to the root note (F) of the iv chord in measure 10. Dale then proves his worth in measure 10 as he dynamically drops down to string 5 with the 6th (D) note nailed dead on and bent a bluesy half step to the bluesier ♭7th note (E♭). Taking a welcome breather in measure 11, he further emphasizes his dynamic side by allowing just the root note (C) to sustain for the duration of the measure.

Performance Tip: If you play the root notes in each measure with your ring finger you will be in an advantageous position to access virtually any and all the other notes that may appear. Bend the D notes in measure 10 by pulling down with your ring finger.

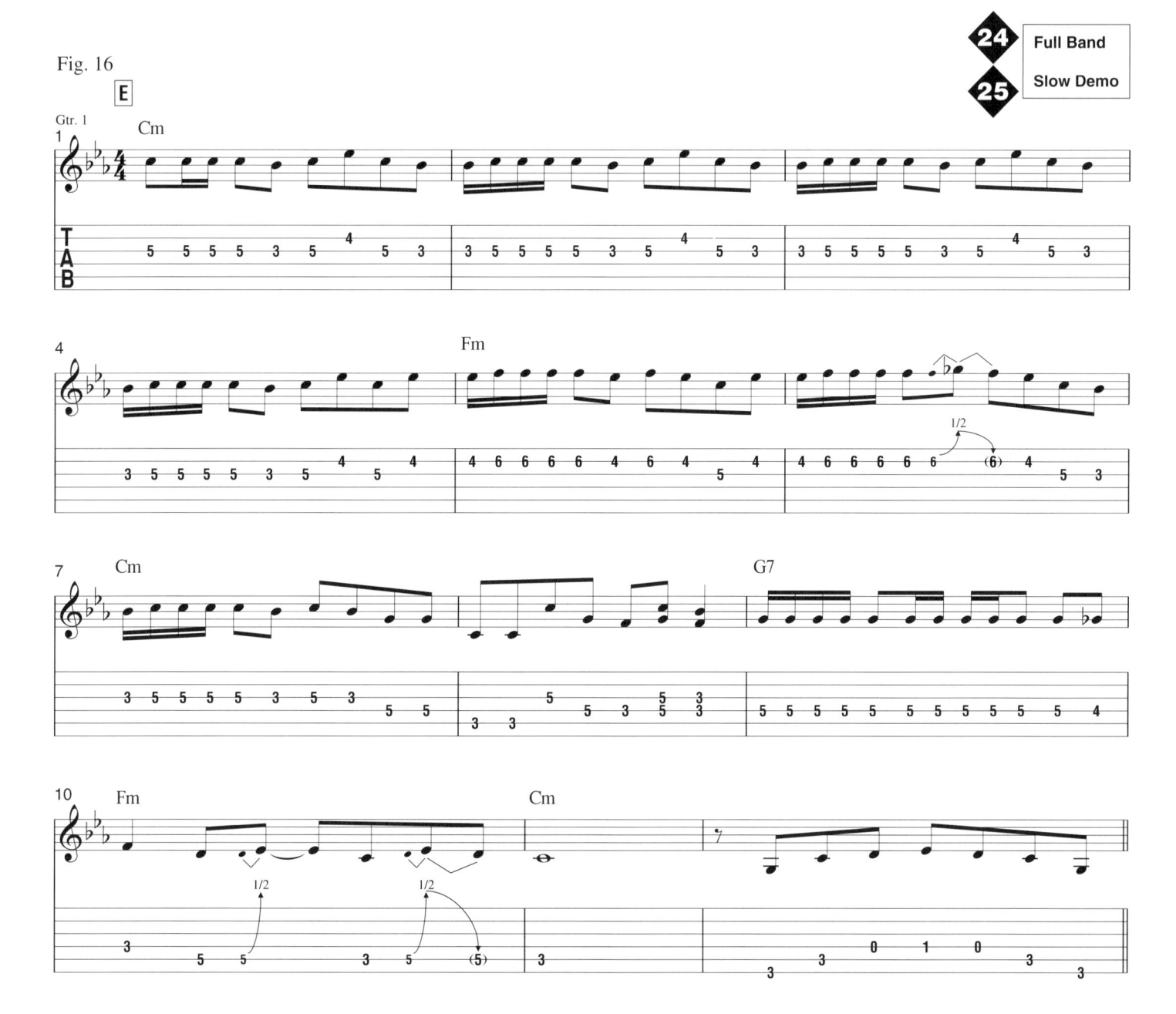

SURF CITY

Words and Music by Brian Wilson and Jan Berry
Recorded by Jan and Dean in 1963

Though hardly ignored in the history of surf music, Jan (Berry) & Dean (Torrence), that sweet-singing duo, have too often been marginalized and dismissed as pop lightweights. In fact, Berry was a multi-track pioneer who had a significant influence on their more respected compadres, the Beach Boys, while showing Brian Wilson the advantage of using top session cats on record, in effect freeing him up to concentrate on putting together more complex arrangements.

Berry (1941–2004) and Torrence (1940–) met and began singing doo-wop in high school in Southern California during the late 1950s. As Jan & Dean they cut the hit "Baby Talk" in 1959 but tread water for the next three years due to a paucity of good material from their publisher. In 1963, however, they became tight with the newly arrived Beach Boys and benefited from Brian Wilson's songwriting via the #1 "Surf City." Jan & Dean had a new direction and were able to sustain it through 1964 with "Ride the Wild Surf" (#16) at the height of the British Invasion when the surf era was almost over. Berry finally succumbed in 2004 to the poor health that plagued him since his accident on "Dead Man's Curve" (#8 in 1964).

Figure 17 – Intro

Using the last two measures of the verse following the two measures of unaccompanied vocals and drums, the guitarist plays a basic E (V) barre chord. Dig the way measure 4 accelerates the momentum with eighth notes. The approach is simple, but as again and again with surf music, very effective.

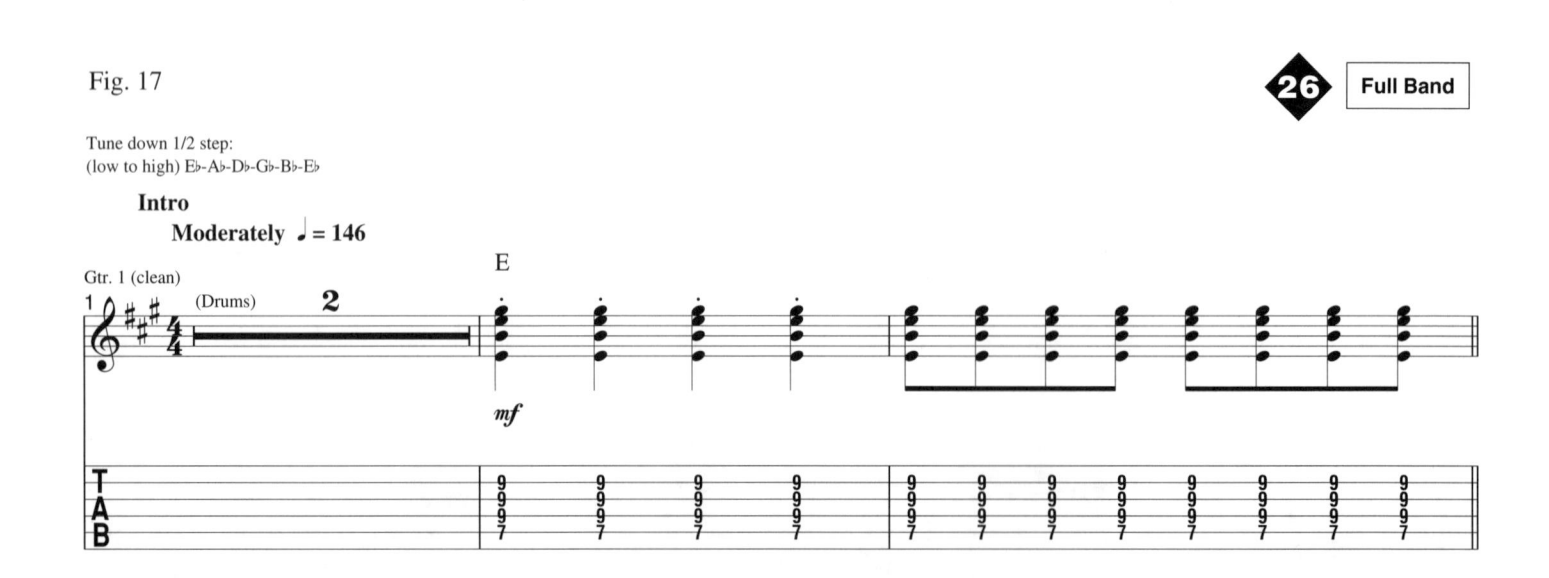

Fig. 17

Tune down 1/2 step:
(low to high) Eb-Ab-Db-Gb-Bb-Eb

Intro
Moderately ♩ = 146

© 1963 (Renewed 1991) SCREEN GEMS-EMI MUSIC INC.
All Rights Reserved   International Copyright Secured   Used by Permission

Figure 18 – Verse

It is a great credit to Jan Berry that, besides his estimable songwriting and arranging skills, he was smart enough to employ the highly skilled services of the "Wrecking Crew" rather than try to keep a band together to back him and Dean. A rotating group of Los Angeles session cats including drummers Hal Blaine and Earl Palmer, bassist Carol Kaye, and guitarists Tommy Tedesco and Glen Campbell, they could not only translate a producer's ideas onto tape, but also add their own creative touches.

The verse of "Surf City" is an odd and unusual 13 measures long and a true testament to Berry's innovative composing. The I–vi vamp in measures 1–8 was already common in rock 'n' roll as well as R&B music, but the IV–ii–♭VII–V chords in measures 9–11 engender hip anticipation with resolution to the V chord. Dig that measures 12 and 13 (V) also function as a vocal hook (as repeated from the intro) and could almost be seen (or heard) as a separate section of the song. Of course, that would still leave an odd, eleven-measure verse! Whatever the theoretical analysis, the result is a clever, well-crafted pop classic.

The guitar line offers up 5ths and 6ths in a rocking boogie pattern "adapted" from Chuck Berry, employing this energetically throughout the majority of the verse section. This is broken up periodically by crinkly, trebly barre chords played in a down-up strum pattern with accentuation on the upbeats. Employ the use of a slight palm mute throughout this section as this serves to tighten up the overall rhythms and maintain the driving surf feel. Note the return to the intro riff in measures 12 and 13 where the guitar locks in for maximum speed through the "curl" at the end of the "ride."

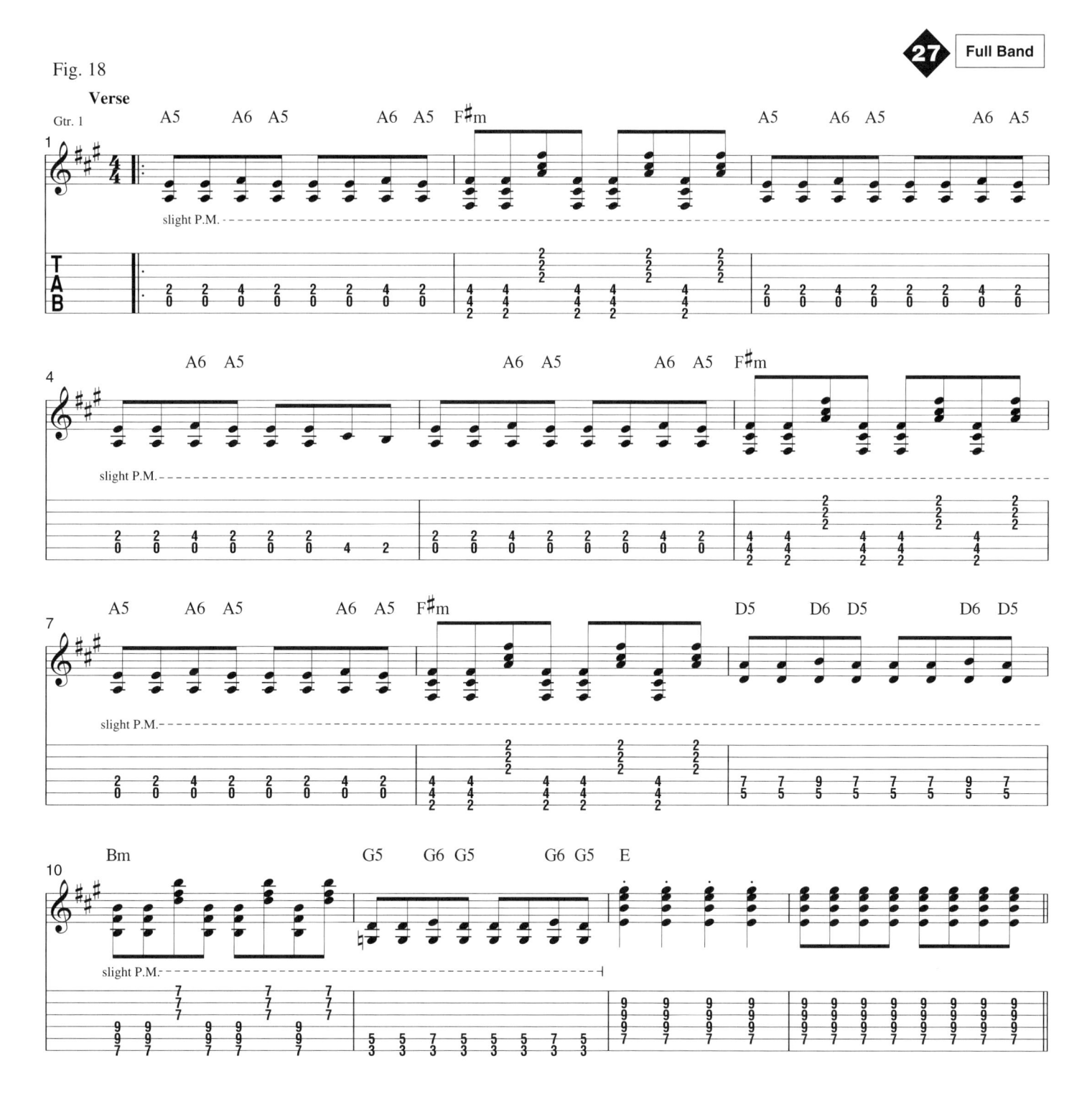

Figure 19 – Chorus

The chorus is a seemingly conventional, twelve-measure, blues-based progression. Ah, but closer inspection reveals that after measures 1–8, Berry and Co. toss a musical curve. In measure 9 where one would expect the V (E) chord, the bIII (C) appears instead, followed by a move up a 4th to the bVI (F) in measure 10. Finally, in measures 11 and 12 the V chord makes its long anticipated appearance (a chromatic, half-step down from the bVI) with the "hook" that is virtually the same as the intro and the last two measures of the verse. To belabor the surfing analogy, it could be seen as the equivalent of a surfer cutting back and forth across the wave, slowing down and accelerating in an attempt to keep his momentum going.

Nowhere is the Jan & Dean/Beach Boys connection more obvious than in the way the guitar is arranged in the chorus of "Surf City." Again it keeps the pulse beating with rocking boogie patterns in 5ths and 6ths in measures 1–8. The similarity to "Surfin' Safari" seems more than a little coincidental!

Fig. 19

SURFIN' SAFARI

Words and Music by Brian Wilson and Mike Love
Recorded by the Beach Boys in 1962

For the many kids who lived away from the West Coast, "Surfin' Safari" was their introduction to the highly appealing Southern California teenage beach culture. The Beach Boys, originally known as the Pendletons, had released "Surfin' " in 1961 on the miniscule Candix label, leading to a contract with Capitol Records. "Surfin' Safari" reached #14 with singer David Marks having replaced Al Jardine, who had left the band to attend college. Significantly, the B side was "409," their first "love song" to a car.

Though the Beach Boys were regularly augmented by L.A. studio musicians (the "Wrecking Crew") on record, guitarist Carl Wilson was accomplished enough with his Chuck Berry licks to be allowed to solo. Wilson (1946–1998) also became de facto leader of the band after 1966 as brother Brian's psychological condition deteriorated. In 1980 he left the band to pursue a solo career but returned in 1982, guiding the band to a comeback in 1985. In the nineties he began a project with Robert Lamm of Chicago and Gerry Beckley of America that was finished just before he died and released in 2000 as *Like a Brother*.

Figure 20 – Verse

The eight-measure verse is comprised of two identical four-measure phrases of I (A), IV (D), V (E), and I. True to his roots, Carl (Gtr. 1) buoys the progression with open-string boogie patterns of 5ths and 6ths relative to each change.

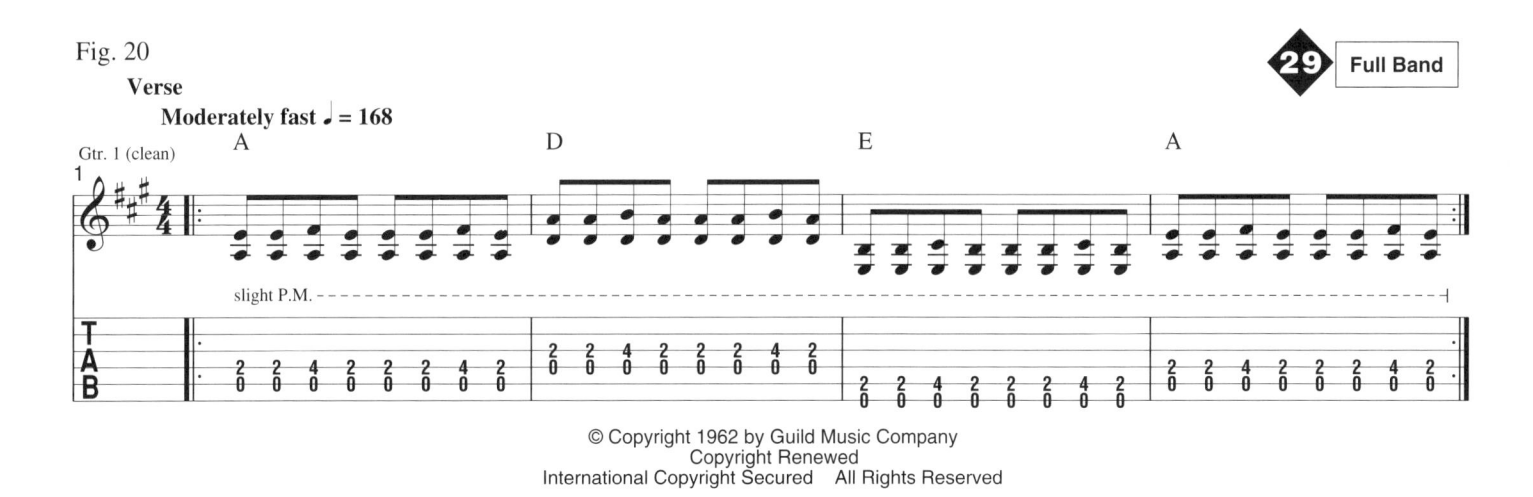

Figure 21 – Chorus

Composer and resident certifiable genius Brian Wilson bent the expected musical rules a bit when he constructed his chorus with thirteen measures, rather than the expected twelve. This is especially intriguing in light of measures 1–8 which follow standard blues practice. Measures 9–13 with V, IV, II (B), V (E), and V however, are the same musically (and lyrically) as the Intro (not shown). Somehow, that extra measure of the V seems perfectly natural. Dig how the move down to the II chord from the IV chord creates extra momentum when the II advances to the V in what could be analyzed as a propulsive V (B)–I (E) move in the key of E.

Fig. 21

Figure 22 – Guitar Solo

The eight-measure solo romps over the same chord progression as the verse. With Gtr. 1 likewise playing the same boogie backup as in the verse, Gtr. 2 (Wilson overdubbed?) uses a ringing combination of duck-walkin' double stops with choice single notes and bends that would have Mr. Berry smiling with benevolence (one hopes!) at one of his prize "students."

Employed as a pickup into measure 1 (I = A), Wilson lays into the classic blues dyad of G/E (♭7th/5th) in the A minor pentatonic scale in seventh position, before finding a home in the fifth position for measures 2–7. Check out that Wilson does not specifically select notes to follow the changing harmony in every single measure. However, he instinctively heads for the F♯/D (3rd/root) and the C (♭7th) and root notes over the IV (D) chord in measures 2 and 6. Granted, he relies heavily on somewhat dissonant E/C (5th/♭3rd) and F♯/D (6th/sus4th) over the I chord in measure 4, but he also emphasizes the root (A) note along with A/E (root/5th) to help define the harmony. The bluesy quarter-step bend of C/F♯ (♭3rd/6th) in measure 5 (I) that resolves to A/E is a Berry specialty derived from the master of modern electric blues guitar, T-Bone Walker.

For the V (E) chord in measure 3 Wilson plays bluesman again with the traditional bend of the D at fret 7 bent up a half step followed by the A that is allowed to ring through beat 3. The E/C (root/♭6th) notes at least contain the root (E), while the A notes on beat 4 anticipate the change back to the I in measure 4. Over the V chord in measure 7, A/F♯ (4th/9th) and A/E (4th/root) combined subtly with E/C to imply the harmony while C♯/A (3rd and root of A) anticipates the I chord in measure 8. Dig the fat triads of E/C♯/A (5th/3rd/root) and F♯/D/A (6th/4th/root) that actually imply an alternating I (A)–IV (D) change as a muscular climax to the solo.

Performance Tip: Hold down the A note on string 1 in measure 3 with your index finger as you barre across strings 3–1. This will enable you to easily access the E/C dyad while using your ring finger to play the D note at fret 7 on string 3. In measure 5, bend the C/F♯ dyad with your ring and pinky fingers (low to high), saving your index for the A/E dyad that follows. In measure 8, play the A triad (low to high) with your ring, middle, and index fingers. Nip the D triad by barring your ring finger quickly over strings 4, 3, and 2.

Fig. 22

SURFIN' U.S.A.

Words and Music by Chuck Berry
Recorded by the Beach Boys in 1963

That the Beach Boys, and especially lead guitarist Carl Wilson, were initially entranced with Chuck Berry was evident from the very beginning. "Surfin' U.S.A.," their second single released five months after the debut of "Surfin' Safari," took the idolatry over the edge. Unbeknownst to most fans and music biz types at the time, it was a virtual rip of Berry's "Sweet Little Sixteen" from 1958. The "Chuckster" was not amused, however, and threatened legal action until he was compensated with royalties and songwriting credits. The joyous youth-anthem helped the Beach Boys on their way to becoming America's most popular rock band in the mid-sixties as it chugged to #3 on the charts—even if the only surfer in the band was Mike Love.

Figure 23 – Intro

The "Boys" were glomming cool licks from everywhere in the early 1960s. The intro to "Surfin' U.S.A." was actually lifted from Duane Eddy's first hit, "Moovin' N' Groovin'," also from that watershed year of 1958. Dig how the simplicity of a root position E♭ (I) major triad with the addition of the sus 4th (A♭) can be phrased to create a classic hook (Gtr. 1).

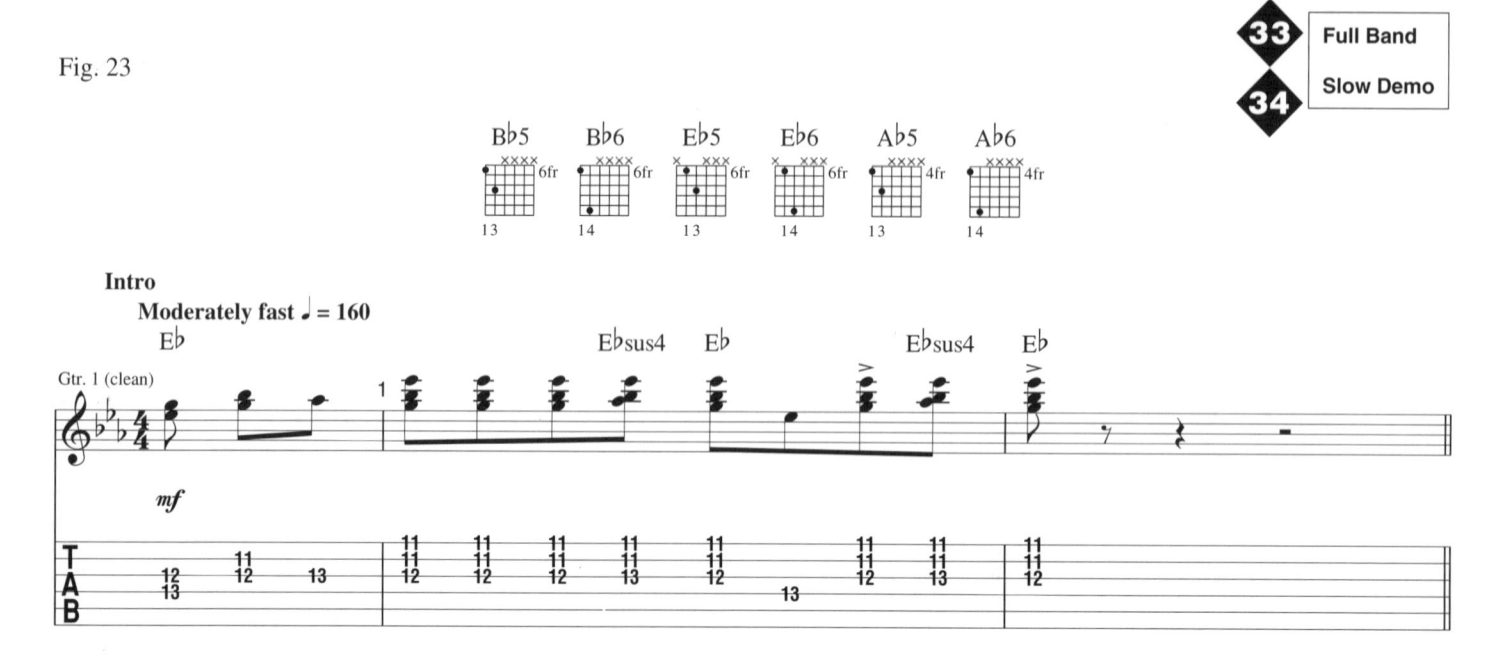

Fig. 23

33 Full Band
34 Slow Demo

Copyright © 1958, 1963 (Renewed) by Arc Music Corporation (BMI) and Isalee Music Inc. (BMI)
International Copyright Secured   All Rights Reserved
Used by Permission

Figure 24 – Verse

The sixteen-measure verses are identical to "Sweet Little Sixteen." Note the dynamic, one-measure rests in measures 2, 4, 6, 8, 10, 12, and 14—a type of rock 'n' roll "call and response." Gtr. 1 plays root position and second-inversion (5th: B♭, on bottom) triads that move I–IV in the V chord measures and measure 9 of the IV chord, along with second-inversion triads for the I (E♭) chord. Gtr. 1 pays tribute to Berry throughout with bass string 5th and 6th boogie patterns appropriate to each chord change.

Performance Tip: The bass string boogie should be played with the index, ring, and pinky fingers. The B♭ and A♭ triads should be fingered (low to high) ring, middle, and index. This will allow you to grab the IV (E♭ in the V chord measures) by quickly flattening your ring finger for a partial barre.

Fig. 24

35 **Full Band**

36 **Slow Demo**
Gtr. 1 meas. 1,9

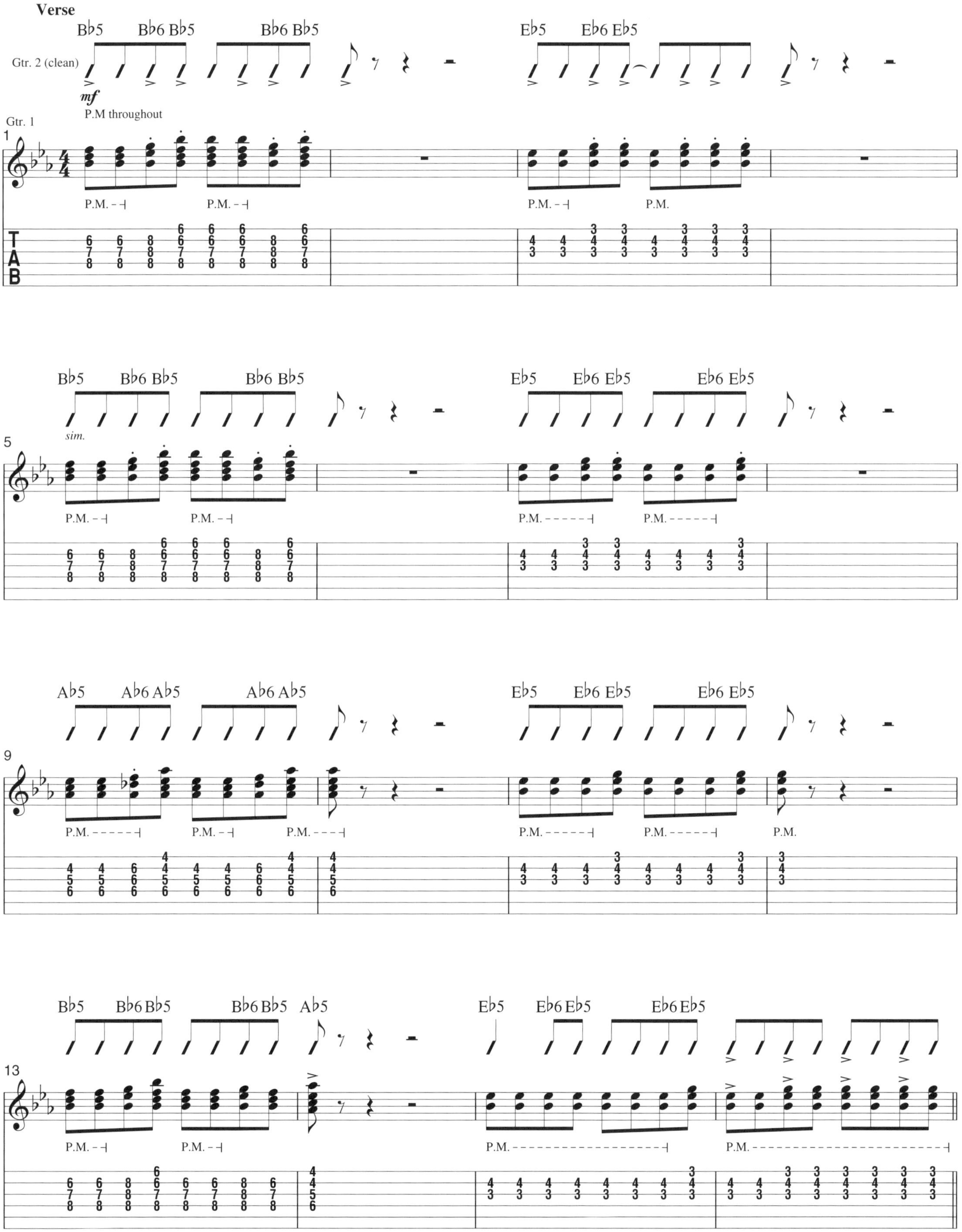

Figure 25 – Guitar Solo

    The organ (not shown) and guitar solos combine for a twelve-measure instrumental break, with the axe of Wilson (Gtr. 1) taking it out on the last four. Over the IV chord (A♭) and I (E♭) chords for two measures each, a double-stoppin', duck walkin' riff is spun that is as energy-packed and memorable as it is brief. For the IV chord in measure 1 Wilson plays G♭/E♭ (♭7th and 5th) dyads, implying a little tension with an A♭ dominant tonality that resolves to the classic Chuck Berry 4th (A♭/E♭) in measure 2.

    Maintaining the concept, Gtr. 1 moves in a parallel fashion up to eleventh position with the chord change (I) for the E♭/B♭ dyad in measure 3. Rocking in the root position of the E♭ blues scale (with a ringing Fender tone) he ripples a half-step bend of A♭ (4th) to A (♭5th) in measure 4 and then interprets a traditional blues move of the 4th bent one-half step to the blues note ♭5th (A♮), released and followed by the ♭3rd (G♭) and resolved to the root (E♭) in measure 4.

Performance Tip: In measure 1, play the G♭/E♭ dyad with your ring and index, low to high, followed by the A♭/E♭ with your index as a barre in measure 2.

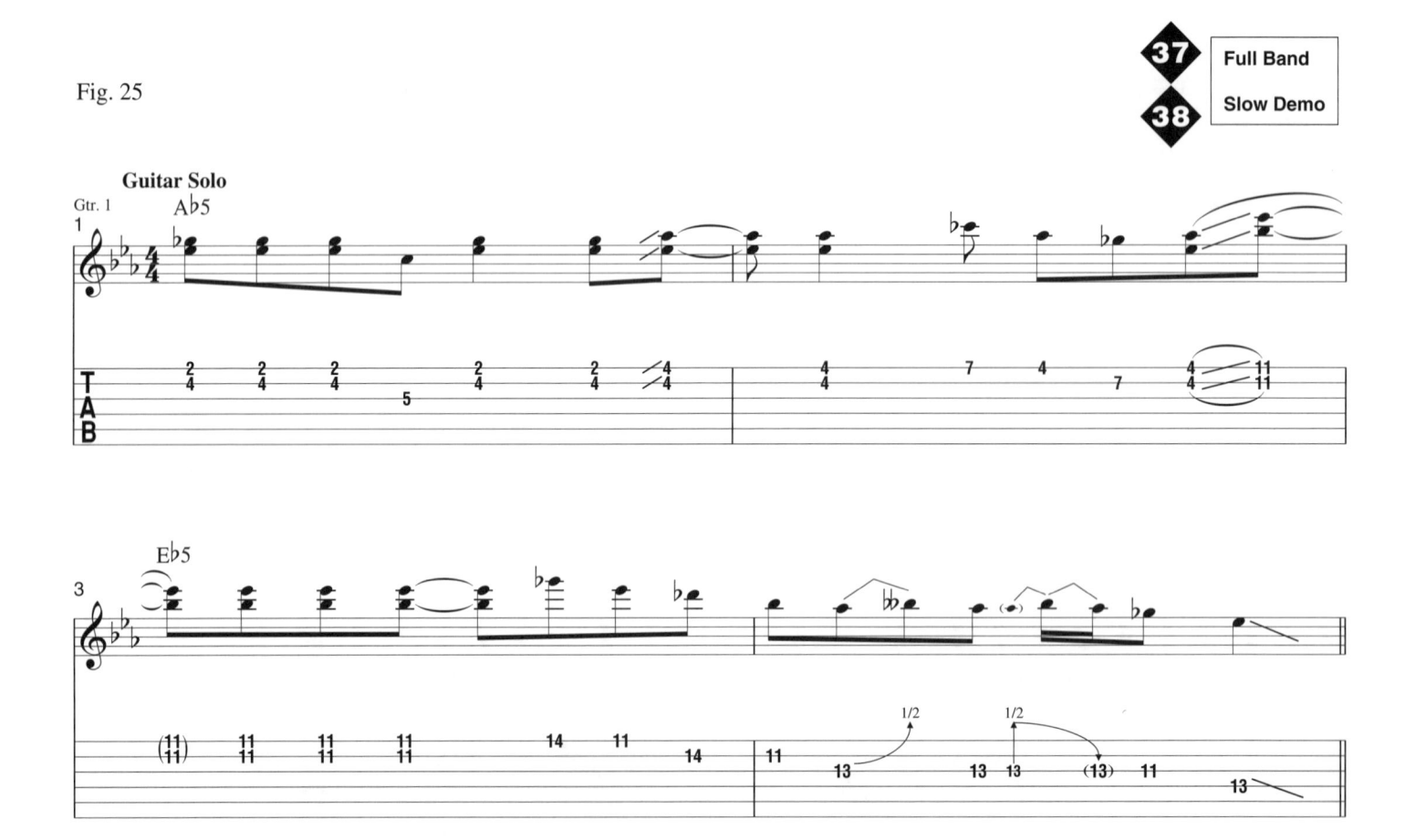

THE WEDGE

By Dick Dale
Recorded by Dick Dale and the Del-Tones in 1963

"The Wedge" was named after a treacherous surfing spot at the tip of the Balboa Peninsula in Newport Beach, California that was famous for its 18–20 foot waves. Released in late 1963, it falls into the Dick Dale category of "exotic" and haunting minor key melodies that recalls "Miserlou" without being totally derivative.

Figure 26 – Rehearsal Letter B

Like the Ventures' "Walk Don't Run" from 1960, "The Wedge" has what functions as a verse (Letter B) and a bridge (Letter C) that repeat as Letters D and E, respectively (not shown). Rehearsal Letter B is twelve measures long but is not a 12-bar blues progression. Instead, it is divided into two six-measure sequences of i (Am), i, i–♭III (G)–♭VI (F), V (E)–♭VI, V, V. Observe how measures 3 and 4 are in 6/4 time, allowing for the F, G, and F changes to squeeze in at two beats each.

Somewhat unusual for an early Dick Dale tune, "The Wedge" has a rhythm guitar part (Gtr. 2) consisting mainly of triads on strings 4–1. Meanwhile, under the guise of Gtr. 1, Dale slams out an A Aeolian mode melody on the three bottom bass strings that is also divided into two virtually identical six-measure sections. Though composed most often around the root and 5th notes, in measures 3 and 9 (Am–G–F) he employs 3rds to create a line that resolves satisfyingly to the root (E) of the following E7 chord that will have you seeing camel caravans in your sleep.

Performance Tip: For Gtr. 1, try playing all the notes at fret 7 with the index, the ones at fret 10 with the pinky, the ones at fret 9 with the ring, and the ones at fret 8 with the middle finger.

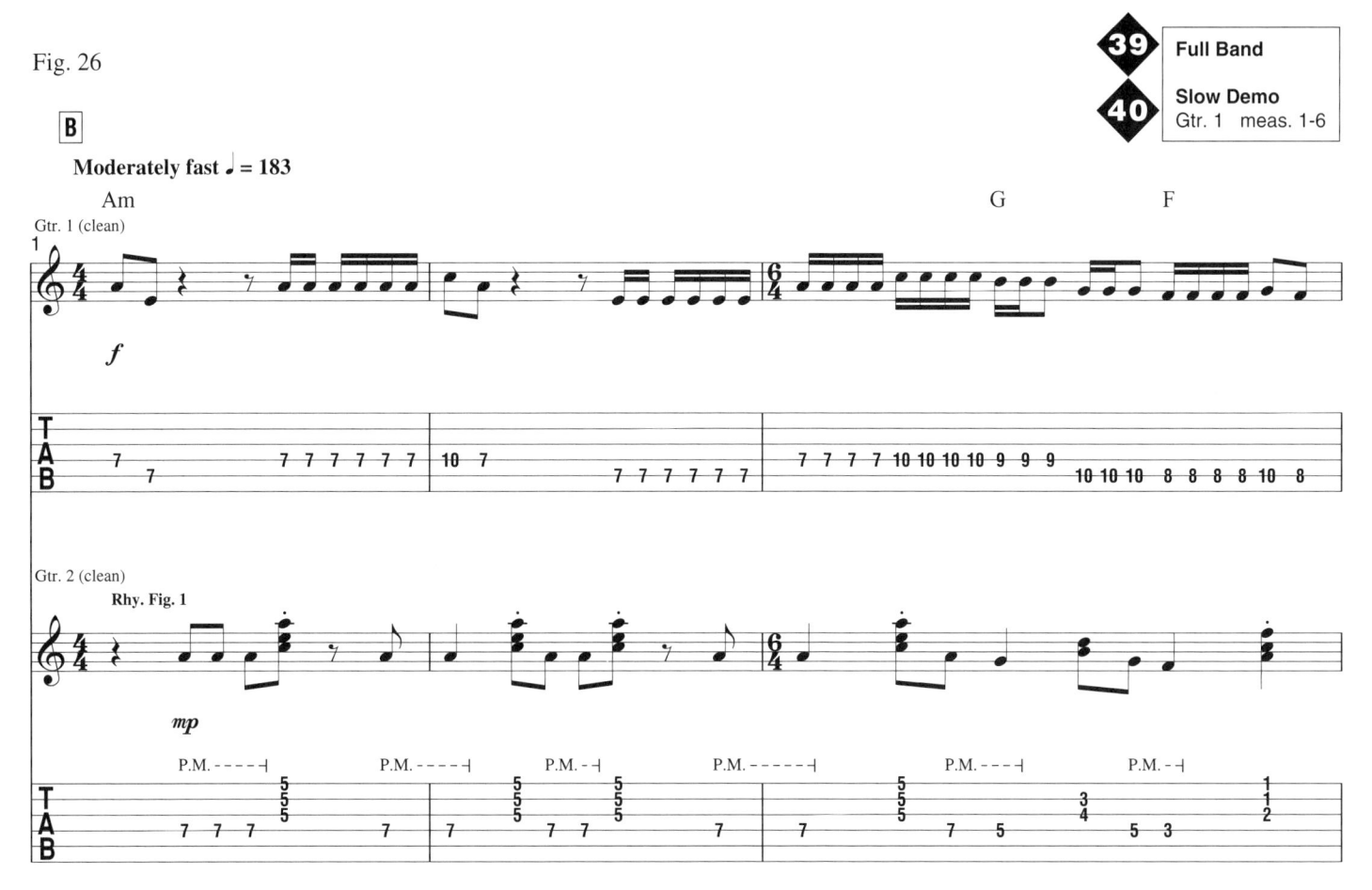

Copyright © 1962 Surf Beat Music (ASCAP)
Copyright Renewed
All Rights Reserved Used by Permission

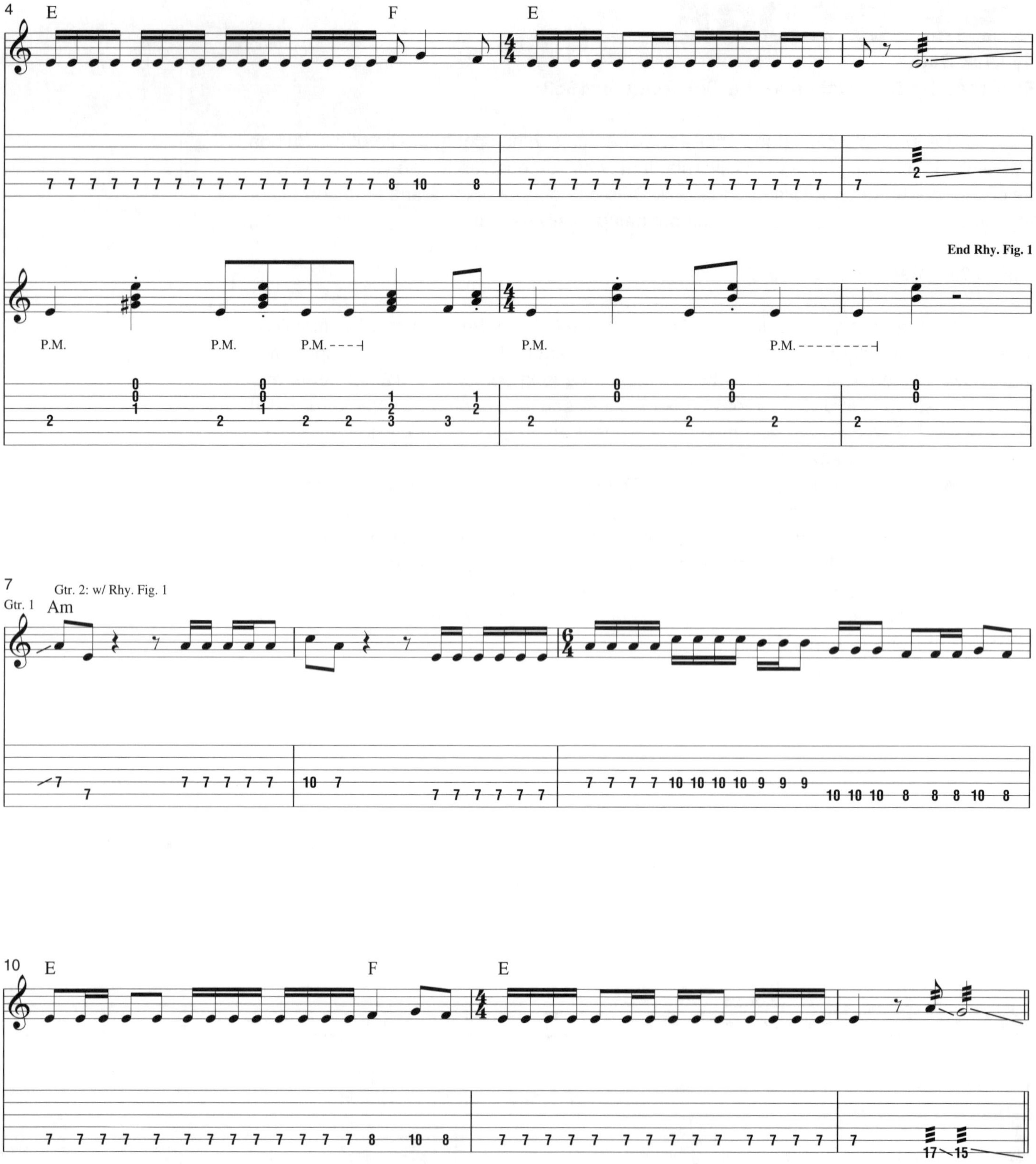
E
F
E
End Rhy. Fig. 1
P.M.
P.M.
P.M.
P.M.
P.M.
Gtr. 2: w/ Rhy. Fig. 1
Gtr. 1
Am
E
F
E

Figure 27 – Rehearsal Letter C

The belly dancers join the vision of a caravan in Rehearsal Letter C as Dale steps up to the treble strings. The thirty-measure section (measures 27–30 contain a rest and the drum intro) follows a clever format that seems to bend time as each one of the three phrases contains a different number of measures.

While Gtr. 2 comps E7 chords and triads similar to Letter B, Gtr. 1 continues to mine the A Aeolian mode around the first position for melodies redolent of frankincense and myrrh. Always cognizant of his chord changes, even if there are only two, Dale weaves lines for the E7 chord with strings 2 (B: 5th) and 1 (E: root) open along with the ♭7th (D) and the tonality-defining major 3rd (G♯) in measure 9. Over the Am chords he emphasizes most prominently the ♭3rd (C) in conjunction with the root (A).

Fascinating anomalies exist, however, that add immeasurably to the onrushing power of the tune. Dale proudly proclaims his ignorance of scales, yet he instinctively and intuitively goes to surprising places that a schooled musician might overlook or dismiss as not feasible. For example, in measure 15 (Am) he rips on the ♭5th (E♭) as a way of building to the root (E) note in measure 16 (E7). Check out the snaky, implied E Phrygian mode in measure 17 (E7) via the ♭2nd (F) and ♭3rd (G) notes. In measures 20, 23, and 24 (Am) he descends the A Aeolian mode but adds the major 7th (G♯) from the harmonic minor scale in lieu of the ♭7th (G) note.

Performance Tip: If you barre across fret 7 with the index finger for the E7, it will be a simple matter to slip down to fret 5 to barre the Am voicing.

7
E7
let ring
End Rhy. Fig. 2
P.M.
10
Gtr. 1
Gtr. 2: w/ Rhy. Fig. 2
Am
let ring
13
16
E7

43

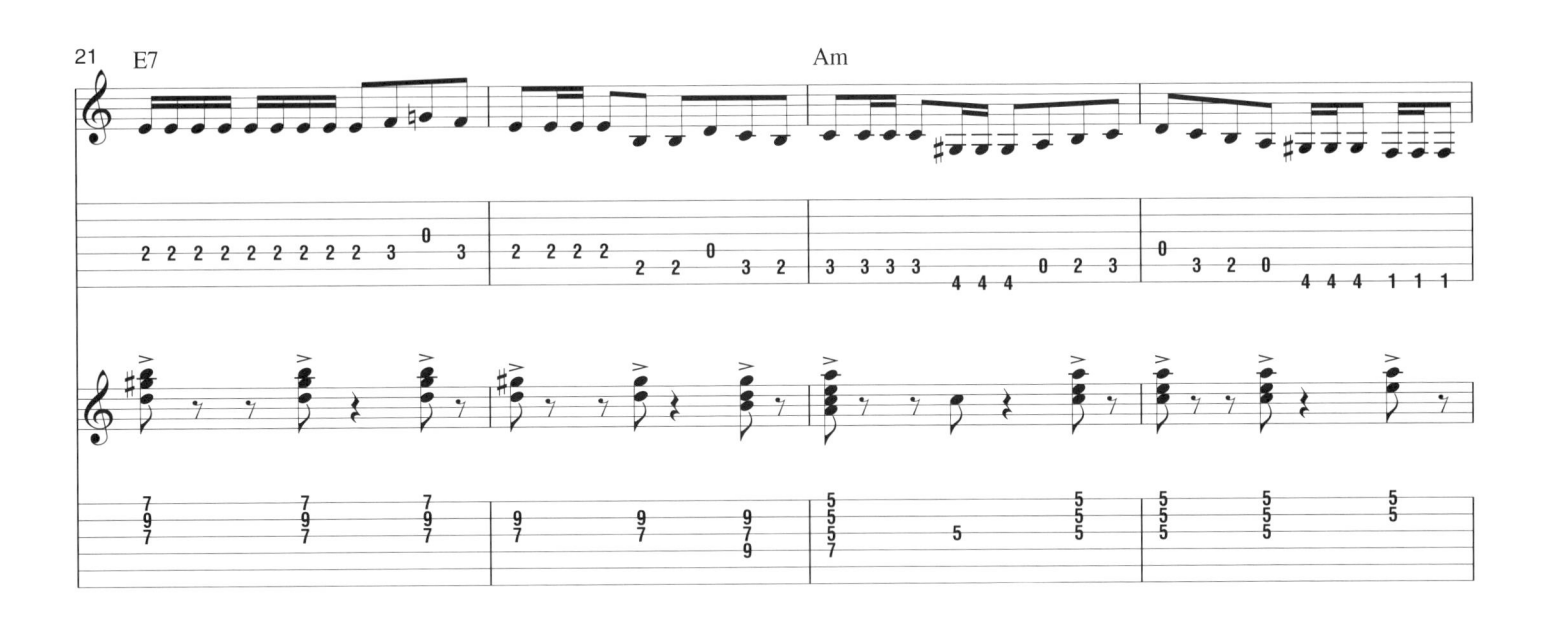

Guitar Notation Legend

Guitar Music can be notated three different ways: on a *musical staff*, in *tablature*, and in *rhythm slashes*.

RHYTHM SLASHES are written above the staff. Strum chords in the rhythm indicated. Use the chord diagrams found at the top of the first page of the transcription for the appropriate chord voicings. Round noteheads indicate single notes.

THE MUSICAL STAFF shows pitches and rhythms and is divided by bar lines into measures. Pitches are named after the first seven letters of the alphabet.

TABLATURE graphically represents the guitar fingerboard. Each horizontal line represents a string, and each number represents a fret.

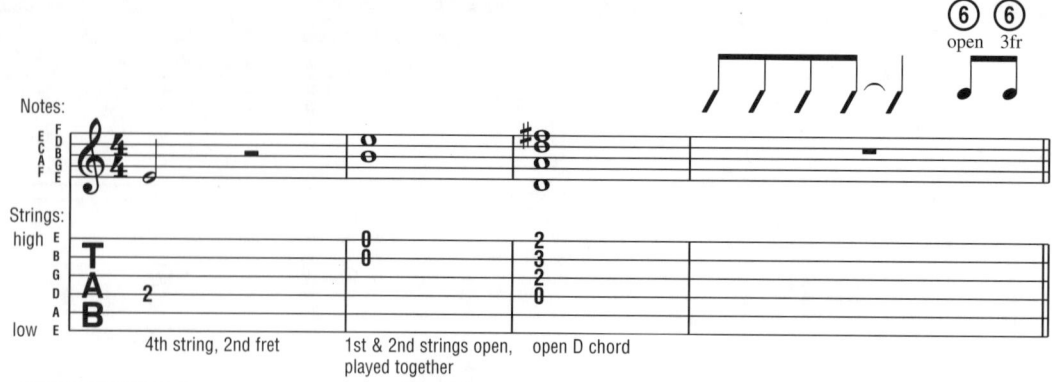

HALF-STEP BEND: Strike the note and bend up 1/2 step.

WHOLE-STEP BEND: Strike the note and bend up one step.

GRACE NOTE BEND: Strike the note and immediately bend up as indicated.

SLIGHT (MICROTONE) BEND: Strike the note and bend up 1/4 step.

BEND AND RELEASE: Strike the note and bend up as indicated, then release back to the original note. Only the first note is struck.

PRE-BEND: Bend the note as indicated, then strike it.

VIBRATO: The string is vibrated by rapidly bending and releasing the note with the fretting hand.

WIDE VIBRATO: The pitch is varied to a greater degree by vibrating with the fretting hand.

HAMMER-ON: Strike the first (lower) note with one finger, then sound the higher note (on the same string) with another finger by fretting it without picking.

PULL-OFF: Place both fingers on the notes to be sounded. Strike the first note and without picking, pull the finger off to sound the second (lower) note.

LEGATO SLIDE: Strike the first note and then slide the same fret-hand finger up or down to the second note. The second note is not struck.

SHIFT SLIDE: Same as legato slide, except the second note is struck.

TRILL: Very rapidly alternate between the notes indicated by continuously hammering on and pulling off.

TAPPING: Hammer ("tap") the fret indicated with the pick-hand index or middle finger and pull off to the note fretted by the fret hand.

NATURAL HARMONIC: Strike the note while the fret-hand lightly touches the string directly over the fret indicated.

PINCH HARMONIC: The note is fretted normally and a harmonic is produced by adding the edge of the thumb or the tip of the index finger of the pick hand to the normal pick attack.

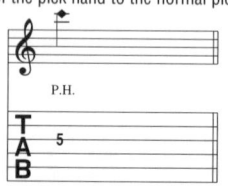

PICK SCRAPE: The edge of the pick is rubbed down (or up) the string, producing a scratchy sound.

MUFFLED STRINGS: A percussive sound is produced by laying the fret hand across the string(s) without depressing, and striking them with the pick hand.

PALM MUTING: The note is partially muted by the pick hand lightly touching the string(s) just before the bridge.

RAKE: Drag the pick across the strings indicated with a single motion.

TREMOLO PICKING: The note is picked as rapidly and continuously as possible.

VIBRATO BAR DIVE AND RETURN: The pitch of the note or chord is dropped a specified number of steps (in rhythm) then returned to the original pitch.

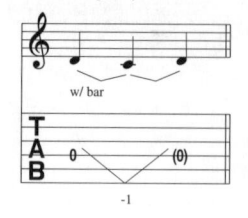

VIBRATO BAR SCOOP: Depress the bar just before striking the note, then quickly release the bar.

VIBRATO BAR DIP: Strike the note and then immediately drop a specified number of steps, then release back to the original pitch.

44

GUITAR *signature licks*

Signature Licks book/CD packs provide a step-by-step breakdown of "right from the record" riffs, licks, and solos so you can jam along with your favorite bands. They contain performance notes and an overview of each artist's or group's style, with note-for-note transcriptions in notes and tab. The CDs feature full-band demos at both normal and slow speeds.

BEST OF ACOUSTIC GUITAR
00695640 .... $19.95

AEROSMITH 1973-1979
00695106 .... $22.95

AEROSMITH 1979-1998
00695219 .... $22.95

BEST OF AGGRO-METAL
00695592 .... $19.95

BEST OF CHET ATKINS
00695752 .... $22.95

THE BEACH BOYS DEFINITIVE COLLECTION
00695683 .... $22.95

BEST OF THE BEATLES FOR ACOUSTIC GUITAR
00695453 .... $22.95

THE BEATLES BASS
00695283 .... $22.95

THE BEATLES FAVORITES
00695096 .... $24.95

THE BEATLES HITS
00695049 .... $24.95

BEST OF GEORGE BENSON
00695418 .... $22.95

BEST OF BLACK SABBATH
00695249 .... $22.95

BEST OF BLINK 182
00695704 .... $22.95

BEST OF BLUES GUITAR
00695846 .... $19.95

BLUES GUITAR CLASSICS
00695177 .... $19.95

BLUES/ROCK GUITAR MASTERS
00695348 .... $19.95

BEST OF CHARLIE CHRISTIAN
00695584 .... $22.95

BEST OF ERIC CLAPTON
00695038 .... $24.95

ERIC CLAPTON – THE BLUESMAN
00695040 .... $22.95

ERIC CLAPTON – FROM THE ALBUM UNPLUGGED
00695250 .... $24.95

BEST OF CREAM
00695251 .... $22.95

DEEP PURPLE – GREATEST HITS
00695625 .... $22.95

THE DOORS
00695373 .... $22.95

FAMOUS ROCK GUITAR SOLOS
00695590 .... $19.95

BEST OF FOO FIGHTERS
00695481 .... $22.95

GREATEST GUITAR SOLOS OF ALL TIME
00695301 .... $19.95

BEST OF GRANT GREEN
00695747 .... $22.95

GUITAR INSTRUMENTAL HITS
00695309 .... $19.95

GUITAR RIFFS OF THE '60S
00695218 .... $19.95

BEST OF GUNS N' ROSES
00695183 .... $22.95

HARD ROCK SOLOS
00695591 .... $19.95

JIMI HENDRIX
00696560 .... $24.95

HOT COUNTRY GUITAR
00695580 .... $19.95

BEST OF JAZZ GUITAR
00695586 .... $24.95

ERIC JOHNSON
00699317 .... $22.95

ROBERT JOHNSON
00695264 .... $22.95

THE ESSENTIAL ALBERT KING
00695713 .... $22.95

B.B. KING – THE DEFINITIVE COLLECTION
00695635 .... $22.95

THE KINKS
00695553 .... $22.95

BEST OF KISS
00699413 .... $22.95

MARK KNOPFLER
00695178 .... $22.95

BEST OF YNGWIE MALMSTEEN
00695669 .... $22.95

BEST OF PAT MARTINO
00695632 .... $22.95

MEGADETH
00695041 .... $22.95

WES MONTGOMERY
00695387 .... $22.95

BEST OF NIRVANA
00695483 .... $24.95

THE OFFSPRING
00695852 .... $24.95

VERY BEST OF OZZY OSBOURNE
00695431 .... $22.95

BEST OF JOE PASS
00695730 .... $22.95

PINK FLOYD – EARLY CLASSICS
00695566 .... $22.95

THE POLICE
00695724 .... $22.95

THE GUITARS OF ELVIS
00696507 .... $22.95

BEST OF QUEEN
00695097 .... $22.95

BEST OF RAGE AGAINST THE MACHINE
00695480 .... $22.95

RED HOT CHILI PEPPERS
00695173 .... $22.95

RED HOT CHILI PEPPERS – GREATEST HITS
00695828 .... $24.95

BEST OF DJANGO REINHARDT
00695660 .... $22.95

BEST OF ROCK 'N' ROLL GUITAR
00695559 .... $19.95

BEST OF ROCKABILLY GUITAR
00695785 .... $19.95

THE ROLLING STONES
00695079 .... $22.95

BEST OF JOE SATRIANI
00695216 .... $22.95

BEST OF SILVERCHAIR
00695488 .... $22.95

BEST OF SOUTHERN ROCK
00695560 .... $19.95

ROD STEWART
00695663 .... $22.95

BEST OF SYSTEM OF A DOWN
00695788 .... $22.95

STEVE VAI
00673247 .... $22.95

STEVE VAI – ALIEN LOVE SECRETS: THE NAKED VAMPS
00695223 .... $22.95

STEVE VAI – FIRE GARDEN: THE NAKED VAMPS
00695166 .... $22.95

STEVE VAI – THE ULTRA ZONE: NAKED VAMPS
00695684 .... $22.95

STEVIE RAY VAUGHAN
00699316 .... $24.95

THE GUITAR STYLE OF STEVIE RAY VAUGHAN
00695155 .... $24.95

BEST OF THE VENTURES
00695772 .... $19.95

THE WHO
00695561 .... $22.95

BEST OF ZZ TOP
00695738 .... $22.95

Complete descriptions and songlists online!

FOR MORE INFORMATION, SEE YOUR LOCAL MUSIC DEALER, OR WRITE TO:

HAL•LEONARD® CORPORATION
7777 W. BLUEMOUND RD. P.O. BOX 13819 MILWAUKEE, WI 53213

www.halleonard.com
Prices, contents and availability subject to change without notice.

RECORDED VERSIONS
The Best Note-For-Note Transcriptions Available

ALL BOOKS INCLUDE TABLATURE

00690501	Adams, Bryan – Greatest Hits	$19.95
00692015	Aerosmith – Greatest Hits	$22.95
00690178	Alice in Chains – Acoustic	$19.95
00690387	Alice in Chains – Nothing Safe: The Best of the Box	$19.95
00694932	Allman Brothers Band – Volume 1	$24.95
00694933	Allman Brothers Band – Volume 2	$24.95
00694878	Atkins, Chet – Vintage Fingerstyle	$19.95
00690418	Audio Adrenaline, Best of	$17.95
00690609	Audioslave	$19.95
00690366	Bad Company – Original Anthology, Book 1	$19.95
00690503	Beach Boys – Very Best of	$19.95
00690489	Beatles – 1	$24.95
00694929	Beatles – 1962-1966	$24.95
00694930	Beatles – 1967-1970	$24.95
00694832	Beatles – For Acoustic Guitar	$19.95
00690137	Beatles – A Hard Day's Night	$16.95
00690482	Beatles – Let It Be	$16.95
00690632	Beck – Sea Change	$19.95
00694884	Benson, George – Best of	$19.95
00692385	Berry, Chuck	$19.95
00692200	Black Sabbath – We Sold Our Soul for Rock 'N' Roll	$19.95
00690674	Blink-182	$19.95
00690389	Blink-182 – Enema of the State	$19.95
00690523	Blink-182 – Take Off Your Pants & Jacket	$19.95
00690028	Blue Oyster Cult – Cult Classics	$19.95
00690583	Boxcar Racer	$19.95
00690491	Bowie, David – Best of	$19.95
00690451	Buckley, Jeff – Collection	$24.95
00690364	Cake – Songbook	$19.95
00690564	Calling, The – Camino Palmero	$29.95
00690043	Cheap Trick – Best of	$19.95
00690567	Christian, Charlie – Definitive Collection	$19.95
00690590	Clapton, Eric – Anthology	$29.95
00692391	Clapton, Eric – Best of, 2nd Edition	$22.95
00690415	Clapton Chronicles – Best of Eric Clapton	$18.95
00690074	Clapton, Eric – The Cream of Clapton	$24.95
00694869	Clapton, Eric – Unplugged	$22.95
00690162	Clash, Best of The	$19.95
00690494	Coldplay – Parachutes	$19.95
00690593	Coldplay – A Rush of Blood to the Head	$19.95
00694940	Counting Crows – August & Everything After	$19.95
00690401	Creed – Human Clay	$19.95
00690352	Creed – My Own Prison	$19.95
00690551	Creed – Weathered	$19.95
00699521	Cure, The – Greatest Hits	$24.95
00690484	dc Talk – Intermission: The Greatest Hits	$19.95
00690289	Deep Purple, Best of	$17.95
00690563	Default – The Fallout	$19.95
00690384	Di Franco, Ani – Best of	$19.95
00695382	Dire Straits – Sultans of Swing	$19.95
00690347	Doors, The – Anthology	$22.95
00690348	Doors, The – Essential Guitar Collection	$16.95
00690555	Etheridge, Melissa – Best of	$19.95
00690524	Etheridge, Melissa – Skin	$19.95
00690515	Extreme II – Pornograffitti	$19.95
00690235	Foo Fighters – The Colour and the Shape	$19.95
00690595	Foo Fighters – One by One	$19.95
00690394	Foo Fighters – There Is Nothing Left to Lose	$19.95
00690222	G3 Live – Satriani, Vai, Johnson	$22.95
00690338	Goo Goo Dolls – Dizzy Up the Girl	$19.95
00690576	Goo Goo Dolls – Gutterflower	$19.95
00690601	Good Charlotte – The Young and the Hopeless	$19.95
00690591	Griffin, Patty – Guitar Collection	$19.95
00694798	Harrison, George – Anthology	$19.95
00692930	Hendrix, Jimi – Are You Experienced?	$24.95
00692931	Hendrix, Jimi – Axis: Bold As Love	$22.95
00690017	Hendrix, Jimi – Live at Woodstock	$24.95
00690602	Hendrix, Jimi – Smash Hits	$24.95
00660029	Holly, Buddy	$19.95
00690457	Incubus – Make Yourself	$19.95
00690544	Incubus – Morningview	$19.95
00690136	Indigo Girls – 1200 Curfews	$22.95
00694912	Johnson, Eric – Ah Via Musicom	$19.95
00690660	Johnson, Eric – Best of	$19.95
00690271	Johnson, Robert – New Transcriptions	$24.95
00699131	Joplin, Janis – Best of	$19.95
00690427	Judas Priest – Best of	$19.95
00690504	King, Albert – The Very Best of	$19.95
00690444	King, B.B. and Eric Clapton – Riding with the King	$19.95
00690339	Kinks, The – Best of	$19.95
00690614	Lavigne, Avril – Let Go	$19.95
00690525	Lynch, George – Best of	$19.95
00694755	Malmsteen, Yngwie – Rising Force	$19.95
00694956	Marley, Bob – Legend	$19.95
00690548	Marley, Bob – One Love: Very Best of	$19.95
00694945	Marley, Bob – Songs of Freedom	$24.95
00690616	Matchbox 20 – More Than You Think You Are	$19.95
00690239	Matchbox 20 – Yourself or Someone Like You	$19.95
00690382	McLachlan, Sarah – Mirrorball	$19.95
00694952	Megadeth – Countdown to Extinction	$19.95
00694951	Megadeth – Rust in Peace	$22.95
00690495	Megadeth – The World Needs a Hero	$19.95
00690505	Mellencamp, John – Guitar Collection	$19.95
00690562	Metheny, Pat – Bright Size Life	$19.95
00690559	Metheny, Pat – Question and Answer	$19.95
00690611	Nirvana	$22.95
00690189	Nirvana – From the Muddy Banks of the Wishkah	$19.95
00694913	Nirvana – In Utero	$19.95
00694883	Nirvana – Nevermind	$19.95
00690026	Nirvana – Unplugged in New York	$19.95
00690121	Oasis – (What's the Story) Morning Glory	$19.95
00690358	Offspring, The – Americana	$19.95
00690485	Offspring, The – Conspiracy of One	$19.95
00690552	Offspring, The – Ignition	$19.95
00690663	Offspring, The – Splinter	$19.95
00694847	Osbourne, Ozzy – Best of	$22.95
00690547	Osbourne, Ozzy – Down to Earth	$19.95
00690399	Osbourne, Ozzy – Ozzman Cometh	$19.95
00694855	Pearl Jam – Ten	$19.95
00690439	Perfect Circle, A – Mer De Noms	$19.95
00690499	Petty, Tom – The Definitive Guitar Collection	$19.95
00690424	Phish – Farmhouse	$19.95
00690240	Phish – Hoist	$19.95
00690607	Phish – Round Room	$19.95
00690331	Phish – Story of the Ghost	$19.95
00690642	Pillar – Fireproof	$19.95
00690428	Pink Floyd – Dark Side of the Moon	$19.95
00690546	P.O.D. – Satellite	$19.95
00693864	Police, The – Best of	$19.95
00690299	Presley, Elvis – Best of Elvis: The King of Rock 'n' Roll	$19.95
00694975	Queen – Greatest Hits	$24.95
00694910	Rage Against the Machine	$19.95
00690145	Rage Against the Machine – Evil Empire	$19.95
00690426	Ratt – Best of	$19.95
00690055	Red Hot Chili Peppers – Bloodsugarsexmagik	$19.95
00690584	Red Hot Chili Peppers – By the Way	$19.95
00690379	Red Hot Chili Peppers – Californication	$19.95
00690090	Red Hot Chili Peppers – One Hot Minute	$22.95
00690511	Reinhardt, Django – Definitive Collection	$19.95
00690643	Relient K – Two Lefts Don't Make a Right...But Three Do	$19.95
00690014	Rolling Stones – Exile on Main Street	$24.95
00690631	Rolling Stones – Guitar Anthology	$24.95
00690600	Saliva – Back Into Your System	$19.95
00690031	Santana's Greatest Hits	$19.95
00690566	Scorpions – Best of	$19.95
00690604	Seger, Bob – Guitar Collection	$19.95
00690419	Slipknot	$19.95
00690530	Slipknot – Iowa	$19.95
00690385	Sonicflood	$19.95
00690021	Sting – Fields of Gold	$19.95
00690597	Stone Sour	$19.95
00690520	Styx Guitar Collection	$19.95
00690519	Sum 41 – All Killer No Filler	$19.95
00690612	Sum 41 – Does This Look Infected?	$19.95
00690425	System of a Down	$19.95
00690606	System of a Down – Steal This Album	$19.95
00690531	System of a Down – Toxicity	$19.95
00694824	Taylor, James – Best of	$16.95
00690238	Third Eye Blind	$19.95
00690580	311 – From Chaos	$19.95
00690295	Tool – Aenima	$19.95
00690654	Train – Best of	$19.95
00690039	Vai, Steve – Alien Love Secrets	$24.95
00690392	Vai, Steve – The Ultra Zone	$19.95
00690370	Vaughan, Stevie Ray and Double Trouble – The Real Deal: Greatest Hits Volume 2	$22.95
00690116	Vaughan, Stevie Ray – Guitar Collection	$24.95
00660058	Vaughan, Stevie Ray – Lightnin' Blues 1983-1987	$24.95
00690550	Vaughan, Stevie Ray and Double Trouble – Live at Montreux 1982 & 1985	$24.95
00694835	Vaughan, Stevie Ray – The Sky Is Crying	$22.95
00690015	Vaughan, Stevie Ray – Texas Flood	$19.95
00694789	Waters, Muddy – Deep Blues	$24.95
00690071	Weezer (The Blue Album)	$19.95
00690516	Weezer (The Green Album)	$19.95
00690579	Weezer – Maladroit	$19.95
00690286	Weezer – Pinkerton	$19.95
00694447	Who, The – Best of	$24.95
00690640	Wilcox, David – Anthology 2000-2003	$19.95
00690320	Williams, Dar – Best of	$17.95
00690596	Yardbirds, The – Best of	$19.95
00690443	Zappa, Frank – Hot Rats	$19.95
00690589	ZZ Top Guitar Anthology	$22.95

Prices and availability subject to change without notice. Some products may not be available outside the U.S.A.

FOR A COMPLETE LIST OF GUITAR RECORDED VERSIONS TITLES, SEE YOUR LOCAL MUSIC DEALER, OR WRITE TO:

HAL•LEONARD CORPORATION
7777 W. BLUEMOUND RD. P.O. BOX 13819 MILWAUKEE, WI 53213

Visit Hal Leonard online at www.halleonard.com   0104

GUITAR PLAY-ALONG

This series will help you play your favorite songs quickly and easily. Just follow the tab and listen to the CD to hear how the guitar should sound, and then play along using the separate backing tracks. Mac or PC users can also slow down the tempo by using the CD in their computer. The melody and lyrics are also included in the book so that you can sing or simply follow along.

INCLUDES TAB

VOL. 1 – ROCK GUITAR   00699570 / $12.95
Day Tripper • Message in a Bottle • Refugee • Shattered • Sunshine of Your Love • Takin' Care of Business • Tush • Walk This Way.

VOL. 2 – ACOUSTIC   00699569 / $12.95
Angie • Behind Blue Eyes • Best of My Love • Blackbird • Dust in the Wind • Layla • Night Moves • Yesterday.

VOL. 3 – HARD ROCK   00699573 / $14.95
Crazy Train • Iron Man • Living After Midnight • Rock You Like a Hurricane • Round and Round • Smoke on the Water • Sweet Child O' Mine • You Really Got Me.

VOL. 4 – POP/ROCK   00699571 / $12.95
Breakdown • Crazy Little Thing Called Love • Hit Me with Your Best Shot • I Want You to Want Me • Lights • R.O.C.K. in the U.S.A. • Summer of '69 • What I Like About You.

VOL. 5 – MODERN ROCK   00699574 / $12.95
Aerials • Alive • Bother • Chop Suey! • Control • Last Resort • Take a Look Around (Theme from "M:I-2") • Wish You Were Here.

VOL. 6 – '90S ROCK   00699572 / $12.95
Are You Gonna Go My Way • Come Out and Play • I'll Stick Around • Know Your Enemy • Man in the Box • Outshined • Smells Like Teen Spirit • Under the Bridge.

VOL. 7 – BLUES GUITAR   00699575 / $12.95
All Your Love (I Miss Loving) • Born Under a Bad Sign • Hide Away • I'm Tore Down • I'm Your Hoochie Coochie Man • Pride and Joy • Sweet Home Chicago • The Thrill Is Gone.

VOL. 8 – ROCK   00699585 / $12.95
All Right Now • Black Magic Woman • Get Back • Hey Joe • Layla • Love Me Two Times • Won't Get Fooled Again • You Really Got Me.

VOL. 9 – PUNK ROCK   00699576 / $12.95
All the Small Things • Fat Lip • Flavor of the Weak • I Feel So • Lifestyles of the Rich and Famous • (So) Tired of Waiting for You • Say It Ain't So • Self Esteem.

VOL. 10 – ACOUSTIC   00699586 / $12.95
Here Comes the Sun • Landslide • The Magic Bus • Norwegian Wood (This Bird Has Flown) • Pink Houses • Space Oddity • Tangled Up in Blue • Tears in Heaven.

VOL. 11 – EARLY ROCK   00699579 / $12.95
Fun, Fun, Fun • Hound Dog • Louie, Louie • No Particular Place to Go • Oh, Pretty Woman • Rock Around the Clock • Under the Boardwalk • Wild Thing.

VOL. 12 – POP/ROCK   00699587 / $12.95
867-5309/Jenny • Every Breath You Take • Money for Nothing • Rebel, Rebel • Run to You • Ticket to Ride • Wonderful Tonight • You Give Love a Bad Name.

VOL. 13 – FOLK ROCK   00699581 / $12.95
Annie's Song • Leaving on a Jet Plane • Suite: Judy Blue Eyes • This Land Is Your Land • Time in a Bottle • Turn! Turn! Turn! • You've Got a Friend • You've Got to Hide Your Love Away.

VOL. 14 – BLUES ROCK   00699582 / $14.95
Blue on Black • Crossfire • Cross Road Blues (Crossroads) • The House Is Rockin' • La Grange • Move It on Over • Roadhouse Blues • Statesboro Blues.

VOL. 15 – R&B   00699583 / $12.95
Ain't Too Proud to Beg • Brick House • Get Ready • I Can't Help Myself • I Got You (I Feel Good) • I Heard It Through the Grapevine • My Girl • Shining Star.

VOL. 16 – JAZZ   00699584 / $12.95
All Blues • Bluesette • Footprints • How Insensitive • Misty • Satin Doll • Stella by Starlight • Tenor Madness.

VOL. 17 – COUNTRY   00699588 / $12.95
Amie • Boot Scootin' Boogie • Chattahoochee • Folsom Prison Blues • Friends in Low Places • Forever and Ever, Amen • T-R-O-U-B-L-E • Workin' Man Blues.

VOL. 18 – ACOUSTIC ROCK   00699577 / $14.95
About a Girl • Breaking the Girl • Drive • Iris • More Than Words • Patience • Silent Lucidity • 3 AM.

VOL. 19 – SOUL   00699578 / $12.95
Get Up (I Feel Like Being) a Sex Machine • Green Onions • In the Midnight Hour • Knock on Wood • Mustang Sally • Respect • (Sittin' On) The Dock of the Bay • Soul Man.

VOL. 20 – ROCKABILLY   00699580 / $12.95
Be-Bop-A-Lula • Blue Suede Shoes • Hello Mary Lou • Little Sister • Mystery Train • Rock This Town • Stray Cat Strut • That'll Be the Day.

VOL. 21 – YULETIDE   00699602 / $12.95
Angels We Have Heard on High • Away in a Manger • Deck the Hall • The First Noel • Go, Tell It on the Mountain • Jingle Bells • Joy to the World • O Little Town of Bethlehem.

VOL. 22 – CHRISTMAS   00699600 / $12.95
The Christmas Song (Chestnuts Roasting on an Open Fire) • Frosty the Snow Man • Happy Xmas (War Is Over) • Here Comes Santa Claus • Jingle-Bell Rock • Merry Christmas, Darling • Rudolph the Red-Nosed Reindeer • Silver Bells.

VOL. 23 – SURF   00699635 / $12.95
Let's Go Trippin' • Out of Limits • Penetration • Pipeline • Surf City • Surfin' U.S.A. • Walk Don't Run • The Wedge.

VOL. 24 – ERIC CLAPTON   00699649 / $14.95
Badge • Bell Bottom Blues • Change the World • Cocaine • Key to the Highway • Lay Down Sally • White Room • Wonderful Tonight.

VOL. 25 – LENNON & McCARTNEY 00699642 / $14.95
Back in the U.S.S.R. • Drive My Car • Get Back • A Hard Day's Night • I Feel Fine • Paperback Writer • Revolution • Ticket to Ride.

VOL. 26 – ELVIS PRESLEY   00699643 / $14.95
All Shook Up • Blue Suede Shoes • Don't Be Cruel • Heartbreak Hotel • Hound Dog • Jailhouse Rock • Little Sister • Mystery Train.

VOL. 27 – DAVID LEE ROTH   00699645 / $14.95
Ain't Talkin' 'Bout Love • Dance the Night Away • Just Like Paradise • A Lil' Ain't Enough • Panama • Runnin' with the Devil • Unchained • Yankee Rose.

VOL. 28 – GREG KOCH   00699646 / $14.95
Chief's Blues • Death of a Bassman • Dylan the Villain • The Grip • Holy Grail • Spank It • Tonus Diabolicus • Zoiks.

VOL. 29 – BOB SEGER   00699647 / $14.95
Against the Wind • Betty Lou's Gettin' Out Tonight • Hollywood Nights • Mainstreet • Night Moves • Old Time Rock & Roll • Rock and Roll Never Forgets • Still the Same.

VOL. 30 – KISS   00699644 / $14.95
Cold Gin • Detroit Rock City • Deuce • Firehouse • Heaven's on Fire • Love Gun • Rock and Roll All Nite • Shock Me.

VOL. 31 – CHRISTMAS HITS   00699652 / $12.95
Blue Christmas • Do You Hear What I Hear • Happy Holiday • I Saw Mommy Kissing Santa Claus • I'll Be Home for Christmas • Let It Snow! Let It Snow! Let It Snow! • Little Saint Nick • Snowfall.

VOL. 32 – THE OFFSPRING   00699653 / $14.95
Come Out and Play • Gotta Get Away • Hit That • Million Miles Away • Original Prankster • Pretty Fly (For a White Guy) • Self Esteem • She's Got Issues.

VOL. 33 – ACOUSTIC CLASSICS   00699656 / $12.95
Across the Universe • Babe, I'm Gonna Leave You • Crazy on You • Heart of Gold • Hotel California • Running on Faith • Thick As a Brick • Wanted Dead or Alive.

VOL. 34 – CLASSIC ROCK   00699658 / $12.95
Aqualung • Born to Be Wild • The Boys Are Back in Town • Brown Eyed Girl • Reeling in the Years • Rock'n Me • Rocky Mountain Way • Sweet Emotion.

VOL. 35 – HAIR METAL   00699660 / $12.95
Decadence Dance • Don't Treat Me Bad • Down Boys • Seventeen • Shake Me • Up All Night • Wait • Your Mama Don't Dance.

VOL. 36 – SOUTHERN ROCK   00699661 / $12.95
Can't You See • Flirtin' with Disaster • Hold on Loosely • Jessica • Mississippi Queen • Ramblin' Man • Sweet Home Alabama • What's Your Name.

VOL. 37 – ACOUSTIC METAL   00699662 / $12.95
Fly to the Angels • Hole Hearted • I'll Never Let You Go • Love Is on the Way • Love of a Lifetime • To Be with You • What You Give • When the Children Cry.

VOL. 38 – BLUES   00699663 / $12.95
As the Years Go Passing By • Boom Boom • Cold Shot • Everyday I Have the Blues • Frosty • Further On up the Road • Killing Floor • Texas Flood.

VOL. 39 – '80S METAL   00699664 / $12.95
Bark at the Moon • Big City Nights • Breaking the Chains • Cult of Personality • Lay It Down • Livin' on a Prayer • Panama • Smokin' in the Boys Room.

VOL. 40 – INCUBUS   00699668 / $14.95
Are You In? • Drive • Megalomaniac • Nice to Know You • Pardon Me • Stellar • Talk Shows on Mute • Wish You Were Here.

VOL. 41 – ERIC CLAPTON   00699669 / $14.95
After Midnight • Can't Find My Way Home • Forever Man • I Shot the Sheriff • I'm Tore Down • Pretending • Running on Faith • Tears in Heaven.

VOL. 42 – CHART HITS   00699670 / $12.95
Are You Gonna Be My Girl • Heaven • Here Without You • I Believe in a Thing Called Love • Just Like You • Last Train Home • This Love • Until the Day I Die.

VOL. 43 – LYNYRD SKYNYRD   00699681 / $14.95
Don't Ask Me No Questions • Free Bird • Gimme Three Steps • I Know a Little • Saturday Night Special • Sweet Home Alabama • That Smell • You Got That Right.

Prices, contents, and availability subject to change without notice.

FOR MORE INFORMATION, SEE YOUR LOCAL MUSIC DEALER, OR WRITE TO:

HAL•LEONARD® CORPORATION
7777 W. BLUEMOUND RD. P.O. BOX 13819 MILWAUKEE, WI 53213

Visit Hal Leonard online at www.halleonard.com

0804